To
Ambien

HEIRS TO
DIRTY LINEN AND
HARLEM GHOSTS

Enjoy

[signature]

Also by the author:

The Seasoned Woman Speaks

HEIRS TO DIRTY LINEN AND HARLEM GHOSTS

WHITEWASHING PROHIBITION WITH BLACK SOAP

Kimberly Robison, Milton Washington, and Carmen Mathis

THEDA PALMER SAXTON, PH.D.

BALBOA
PRESS

A DIVISION OF HAY HOUSE

Book cover design by the author

Photographed by Sharell Jeffery-Cazenave

Cover: Kimberly Robison, Milton Washington, Carmen Mathis

Balboa Press books may be ordered through booksellers or by contacting:

Balboa Press
A Division of Hay House
1663 Liberty Drive
Bloomington, IN 47403
www.balboapress.com
1-(877) 407-4847

Because of the dynamic nature of the Internet, any web addresses or links contained in this book may have changed since publication and may no longer be valid. The views expressed in this work are solely those of the author and do not necessarily reflect the views of the publisher, and the publisher hereby disclaims any responsibility for them.

The author of this book does not dispense medical advice or prescribe the use of any technique as a form of treatment for physical, emotional, or medical problems without the advice of a physician, either directly or indirectly. The intent of the author is only to offer information of a general nature to help you in your quest for emotional and spiritual well-being. In the event you use any of the information in this book for yourself, which is your constitutional right, the author and the publisher assume no responsibility for your actions.

Any people depicted in stock imagery provided by Thinkstock are models, and such images are being used for illustrative purposes only. Certain stock imagery © Thinkstock.

ISBN: 978-1-4525-7377-9 (sc)
ISBN: 978-1-4525-7378-6 (hc)
ISBN: 978-1-4525-7376-2 (e)

Library of Congress Control Number: 2013909435

Printed in the United States of America.

Balboa Press rev. date: 12/8/2013

Table of Contents

List of Illustrations

Image # 00
- Cover Photo, Kimberly Robison, Milton Washington, and Carmen Mathis

Image # 01
- 107 West 133rd Street, Mother Shepherd's Speakeasy and Rooming House

Image # 02
- 146 West 133rd Street, Edith's Clam House

Image # 03
- 148 West 133rd Street, Tillie's Kitchen Shack

Image # 04
- 152 West 133rd Street, Brownies Basement

Image # 05
- 154 West 133rd Street, Mexico

Image # 06
- 168 West Street, the Log Cabin (the Pod)

Image # 07
- 169 West 133rd Street, the Nest

Image # 08
- 169 West 133rd Street Nest

Image # 09
- 116th Street and 7th Avenue / Frederick Douglass Boulevard

Image # 10
- 118th Street and St. Nicholas Avenue

Image # 11
- 125th Street and Lenox Avenue / Malcolm X Boulevard, NW corner

Image # 12
- 125th Street and Lenox Avenue / Malcolm X Boulevard, NE corner

Image # 13
- Lenox Avenue / Malcolm X Boulevard, between 126th Street and 127th Street

Image # 14
- Lenox Avenue / Malcolm X Boulevard, between 126th Street and 127 Street

Image #: 15
- 124th and 8th Avenue / Frederick Douglass Boulevard and 124th Street, NW corner

Image # 16
- 125th and 8th Avenue / Frederick Douglass Boulevard and 124th Street, NW corner

Image # 17
- 135th and 7th Avenue / Adam Clayton Powell Boulevard, SW corner

Image # 18
- 8th Avenue between 137th Street and 138th Street

Image # 19
- 145th Street and Bradhurst, SE corner

Image # 20
- 145th Street and Bradhurst, NE corner

Image # 21
- 110th Street Duke Ellington Circle at 5th Avenue / Central Park

Image # 22
- John Hicks Way

Image # 23
- St. Nick's Pub, 149th and St. Nicholas Avenue

Image # 24
- Minton's Playhouse, 118th Street, between 7th Avenue and St. Nicholas Avenue

Image # 25
- Minton's Playhouse, 118th Street, between 7th Avenue and St. Nicholas Avenue

Image # 26
- Lenox Lounge, Lenox Avenue / Malcolm X Boulevard, between 125th Street and 124th Street

Image # 27
- Lenox Lounge, Lenox Avenue / Malcolm X Boulevard between 125th Street and 124th Street

Image # 28
- Renaissance Ballroom, 138th Street, between 7th Avenue and Lenox Avenue

Image # 29
- Harlem Hospital, 135th Street and Lenox Avenue, birthplace of Bill saxton

Image # 30
- Home site of Bill Saxton, 2534 Seventh Avenue

Image # 31
- Home site of Bill Saxton, 2534 Seventh Avenue

Image # 32
- P. S. 90, West 147th Street near Lenox Ave.,Bill Saxton's Elementary school

Image # 33
- Jackie Robinson Park, 148th Street and Bradhurst Avenue

Image #34
- Jackie Robinson Park, 148th Street and Bradhurst Avenue

Image #35
- Theda and Bill, in front of Bill's Place

Image #36
- Charlie Phillips

Image # 37
- Bill Saxton and Sonny Stitt

Image # 38
- Max Roach and Bill Saxton

Image # 39
- Barry Harris, Willie Williams, Clark Terry, Carrie Smith, and Bill Saxton

For My Best Teachers:

Daddy, Theodore Palmer, 1910-1989

Mother, Pauline Palmer, 1913-2009

Brother, Joseph Palmer, 1933-1998

Preface

My life in Harlem spans over half of a century. As a mother, educator, theater and musical director, entrepreneur, landlord, and citizen, I am a participating, primary resource for many of the diverse levels of life in Harlem. Geographically, Harlem has the best location on the island of Manhattan. It is in the center of New York City, all trains connect uptown, it still has hills and valleys, and people of every ethnic group imaginable either work or live in the area.

This writing was kindled by a small spark of curiosity that grew into some heated issues for me when I investigated the background of our speakeasy from the historical documentation of Prohibition and bootlegging. Most written material referred to the lives of white people. Politicians, gangsters, violence, and greed were overriding variables that consumed the lives of all Americans of that era, but little included the effects that these variables had on the lives of my people, except as performers.

Were we looked upon as entertainment, as we were on the Southern plantations fifty years before the alcohol stopped? Did we have families and have relationships as white people? Were we able to own our blues and jazz music? Little is fully explored in this cultural arena.

This is a cursory attempt to weave some of America's history over approximately fifty years of sordid Prohibition history into a single, coarse braid, and it is exciting. My first goal is to intertwine two separate, unequal lives of post-slavery black and white people along a trail with the common Prohibition experience—which leads to Theda's Space, more commonly known as Bill's Place, Harlem's only authentic speakeasy. However, the past is still dictating the current day-to-day lives of the people of Harlem. The face of the occupation has shifted from ignorant, greedy bootleggers of the Prohibition Era to highly educated, greedy businessmen of the gentrification era.

Uncovering the mesh of circumstances and events that shaped the pathway to our acquisition of this particular location for a jazz speakeasy on the notorious Swing Street is a movie script. But you can't make this up.

Timing is everything.

Acknowledgments

To Dr. T. D. Pawley, Chair Emeritus of Speech and Drama at Lincoln University, Jefferson City, Missouri, for giving me the opportunity to sit at the feet of a true master and learn the tools of the theater business, which enabled me to see as an artist and then produce as a professional. My debt to you is deep like the rivers. Thank you.

There are not enough accolades to give to my good friend, Charlie Phillips. He discovered our cultural relevancy as an authentic Harlem speakeasy on Swing Street. Because of Charlie, this writing project became a meaningful journey back in time and across cultural and racial barriers, and it ended up at Bill's Place. This is so typical of his deep commitment to intellectual pursuits. Hopefully, it is worthy of him.

Part One:

THE INCREDIBLE TALE

CHAPTER ONE

White Women Give Birth to Prohibition

Woman conceives, nurtures, and gives birth to new life. Her ability to manifest fresh, new life is one of the natural, phenomenal powers reserved for her. She has the ability to easily give birth to flesh or spiritual concepts; both require conception, nurturing, and delivery. Although it is a time-consuming process, women seem to do it naturally. Giving birth permits them to take ownership of the process, as if it's their private right just because they're women.

Some call it wisdom; others call it mother wit, or women's intuition. Whatever it's called, it doesn't matter. As a young girl, when I would delicately question my mother's or grandmother's judgment of an issue, they had a standard answer: "Because I said so." That was it, end of conversation. "Because I said so" had an authoritative ring to it. That answer was the only and last word to resolve the issue.

My mother said she knew what she knew, and she did not have to qualify it any further. She was also usually right.

They Got Pregnant

Somewhere around the late 1800s, far too many women suffered from what is presently called domestic violence. They had little legal recourse or protection back then. Being on the losing end of the weekend drunken brawls with their husbands regarding paychecks spent in saloons became intolerable. Oftentimes, fights and beatings of women and their children in poor or working-class white families became a common script that was no longer bearable.

Women became impregnated with an idea. Like falling rain, the pregnant notion of power peppered the spirits of women across the country. This awakened a group of women, and their sympathizers found a common cord that connected many of their salient issues into a simplistic concept: no more domestic violence and economic dependency. Essentially, white women demanded to have power over the quality of their lives.

The power of the idea struck with clarity and held salvation in its reins. The alcohol and saloons were the initial culprits. The women identified the enemy. These women wanted the saloons to stop selling alcohol and to close down. It seemed perfectly logical to them that in turn, their husbands would stop drinking and squandering their wages. Almost all women wanted sober and responsible husbands, fathers, and brothers. As a group they were convinced they had the solution to their domestic violence issue. They were willing to nurture and deliver this ideal across the country and see the laws change, even if it meant changing the Constitution.

They conceived a fresh, new lifestyle for themselves and were willing to do whatever was necessary to get the laws changed. To the best of their limited knowledge of the real world, these women honestly thought their social and domestic issues were caused primarily by the excessive drinking of alcohol in saloons. But how were these women to know the severity of the far-reaching and negative, complex ramifications and mayhem that their new idea would unleash in America?

With absolute resolve and newly discovered self-confidence in their mission to fight saloons and alcohol, this initially small group of religious white women forged ahead with fury. They knew they were right. Who could challenge their collective voice of the "Because I said so" mentality of righteousness?

However, tampering with the governing laws of the land to satisfy a growing multitude of well-intentioned women proved to be more than anyone could anticipate. Unknown to these community-minded women, who were ideologically pregnant with a lofty dream that was in reality a maniacal, monstrous embryo, the new brainchild would eventually bring forth to the American scene a live concept of such magnitude that the birthmothers would be powerless to harness it. The intuitive mother wit did not give them a clue that they had conceived a King Kong in Hillsboro, Ohio, 1873. They were sure of one thing: their ideological baby's name would be Prohibition.

Carrying Dreams to Full Term

Their new baby, Prohibition, was absolutely incompatible with America's Constitution. The document was written by all white men and for all white men, to keep democracy stable for their best interests. Historically, race and gender were in ideological conflict in the original democratic structure of America's Constitution, and therefore the document provided settings for ensuing battles. White men gave themselves unquestioned power—

everybody else was invisible. Nonetheless, their women remained true to their intuitive format, and they relentlessly kept pushing forward to deliver the passionate embryo that burned in their bellies. The women would tackle the men and their constitution head-on.

On the other hand, during the same time frame of the late 1800s, black women knew they needed to take action to create a better life for their families. The salient issues of domestic violence and intoxicated husbands that ignited hot political reactions of white women were of no interest to black people in America. White women wanted sober husbands and closed saloons; black women wanted the right to get married and have a husband—and for him to not be lynched by a band of white cowards hiding under white sheets. Each was seeking changes in the Constitution. Each woman wanted power from the white man to gain parity for the improvement of their particular living conditions. Each lived as far apart as imaginable, but within clear vision of each other's predicament.

Although there was no established communication between white women and black women during or after slavery, each was aware of the reality of the white man's abuse and unquestioned power. Historically, they had both felt the brunt of his subtle and often savage anger, and they learned how to placate the white master to get what they could for themselves.

Timing is everything.

America was going through a chain reaction of bipolar political policy swings. It started with the Civil War from 1861 to 1865, and then President Lincoln brought about the abolition of slavery, signing the Emancipation Proclamation on January 1, 1863. In the same year women were staging sit-ins in saloons in Millsboro, Ohio; that was followed closely by President Lincoln's assassination, which placed America into a virtual eggbeater. The climate in the country was in turmoil and confusing for whites and blacks alike. Change had come, and cultural norms were being redesigned. Seeds of discontent landed on new soil and took root.

America's standard, white man's superiority policies were being challenged; it was a perfect time for new ideas to spring forth. Extraordinary women, unknown to each other from different camps, were crossing unconscious paths and going in the same direction of freedom. The black path was a matter of life and death. That of the white woman was of personal self-worth. Each carried the potential to create something new.

Harriet Tubman had already been preparing freed slaves, brought through the Underground Railroad into free Northern schools for training so that they could be productive, free blacks with skills needed in their new urban communities. Susan B. Anthony, an educated Quaker, pioneered white women's right to vote. She knew that the right to vote was the key to real power for the white woman. It is amazing that Harriet and Susan were both born the same year, 1820. Each woman, black and white, was busily preparing her own kind to move forward in the new post-Civil War and post-slavery era in America. Freedom from the slave system and freedom to vote were non-negotiable agendas from the camps of these women.

White, Female, and Angry

White women possessed few rights independently of their white men. Although they were technically free, they were without political and economic power. A white woman lacked a voice; she had no legal power to control her domestic household, and that included her bedroom. Her powerful white husband raped and slept with whomever, wherever and whenever he pleased. The black house slaves gave birth to fair-skinned, blond babies with light eyes and other features that looked like the white woman's husband and their children. The man had no regard for her feelings or pride. The white woman had no vote and owned no land, property, or slaves in her name, but she could claim her fair skin and soft, straight hair. The black man and woman could claim nothing but superior fortitude.

The carnage from the Civil War left the Southern white woman where she was before it started. Her position was only affected in as much as her man's status was changed. In 1865, when slavery was abolished, it served as a conscious wake-up call to her precarious position in America. Blacks from plantations began to migrate away from the Southern farmland to the more industrialized North in search of work, although some remained as sharecroppers.

But for the most part, the most poor and modest economic white rural households were without free domestic services and essentially free field labor. For the first time, some Southern white women had to raise their own children, do daily chores, and maintain all household responsibilities. Because of the formation of the KKK and white citizen organizations, many white households were able to maintain some of slavery's benefits because of sharecropping and detaining blacks for years to work off imaginary fines imposed by sheriffs and judges.

However, many less affluent were forced to become self-reliant. Without the benefit of education, money, or political power to affect social change in their best interests, many white women learned to adapt to new roles forced upon them by circumstances beyond their control. The Civil War and post-slavery aftermath left some whites with few valuable possessions to hold on to. Having white skin was all many Southerners had left to embrace as a superior possession. Likewise, to secure their whiteness further, men created the mystical, highly protected pedestal for their woman to occupy. The white woman, regardless of how poor, uneducated, or physically unattractive, automatically became a psychologically coveted trophy. Possessing the trophy gave all white men, poor and affluent, parity in the illusion of possessing power.

Meanwhile, the black woman was left by the wayside without elevation from her man, who unfortunately forgot that it was his role to do for her what the white man had done for his woman.

However, living on a pedestal was not a comfort zone for the struggling, poorer class of white women. It proved to be a dysfunctional symbol used by Southern mobs to have as a cause for lynching black boys. White women sought substance. In order to sustain their families and stay together, they acquired life skills and became survivors. Much of their energy was put into churches and civic organizations, where they rallied around mutual issues and discovered the power of large, unified numbers. These emerging women organizers sought new ways of solving their common problems. As memberships increased, especially in the small cities, education became a key component in their developing independence. Through education, large numbers of women became aware of how a democratic government was supposed to work, and of the human rights all citizens were entitled to enjoy. The Constitution was now available for reading along with other civics books.

Shared readings and public speaking in front of religious audiences and political forums became tools for the evolving political awareness. White women utilized their organizational skills and personal relationships with their husbands, fathers, brothers, and ministers to influence powerful politicians to push their particular issues forward.

Historically, the early 1900s was a time for curious minds and unleashed new energy to take flight down the road of adventure. The white woman needed a vehicle to push her agenda forward; advocacy for change became her mantra. Banning saloons and alcohol and getting voting rights were adopted as the key issues for the movements' expanding agenda.

How this group of white women climbed off their pedestals and rolled up their sleeves to create the climate to convince politicians to embrace the anti-drinking-law sentiments is an exciting phase of American history. It remains one of the most interesting historical stories of persuasive lobbying.

"Let's Have Our War"

The lesson learned from this early female-driven political coup is to use the power of the perception of a common enemy that threatens the well-being of all members of the organizations, as the point of the attack. It became a moral war of survival. This huge group of disenfranchised and unhappy white women took courageous steps to strengthen and improve the well-being of their families, while increasing the influence of the church doctrine in their communities. Husbands coming home drunk, fighting with their wives, and sometimes beating their children were serious issues for many households. Spending too much of the household money while gambling in saloons, paying for drinks and prostitutes, and spending hours away from home were key common issues around which women rallied.

Saloons, the sites for the consumption of alcohol, became the primary enemies. The women used Christianity as their battle ax against the saloon establishments, to drive their intoxicated husbands at home and the saloons out of business.

In 1873 Hillsboro, Ohio, was the scene of small groups of determined women staging many saloon sit-ins and sit-outs. Ideally, the ladies wore long black dresses with long sleeves, full skirts, and tight collars high around the neck. With very little conversation, a hoard of women would descend upon a saloon location, ready for battle. They boldly carried their Bibles like protective shields. Uninvited, they sat in the center of the saloon floor, perched in chairs, sang hymns, and prayed loudly. If getting inside was not possible, they sat outside the entrance doors in small groups and walked, sang, and yelled at men as they entered.

In rainy weather, they sat under black umbrellas that covered them like tents. The Christian ladies always wore very wide-brimmed bonnets with ties under the chin. Their pale faces were clean, and they hair was compliantly in place; they were stoic and persistent. The saloon owners found them to be a nuisance to the men wanting to drink and have fun with their comrades. Some men left their favorite saloons because their wives, mothers, and sisters were members of the Christian brigade.

Within a short time after the Ohio anti-saloon activity started, a surge of movements cropped up in different parts of the country. The methods and tactics changed, but the enemy remained: saloons and drinking alcohol. Some women gave tea parties in private homes, and some gave speeches in public halls, but the focus was consistent: ban alcohol. They formulated an enemy to attack.

Discovering Political Muscle

The combined energies of Mother Eliza Thompson's Crusade and Carrie Nation (the barroom smasher)—followed by the Woman's Christian Temperance Union, Susan B. Anthony, and Elizabeth Candy Stanton (advocates for women's right to vote), and the Anti-Saloon League—pooled together a mighty force for social change. Their combined numbers were staggering. Politicians were at a loss for how to control this pervasive tidal wave of female determination.

Wayne B. Wheeler, an original Capitol Hill insider lobbyist, had the loyalty of the Anti-Saloon League (ASL), and more important, the ear of spineless and shallow-minded President Warren G. Harding. The women of the ASL had direct influence on the White House level through Wheeler. After deals and promises were made in the name of the common good and decency, Wheeler was able to use his thousands of women supporters as power brokers for change, although they could not vote.

The Pivotal Year of 1919

On January 16, 1919, the Eighteenth Amendment to the Constitution was ratified and essentially gave the women's organizations what they were after: Prohibition. Under the guise of correcting a moral weakness, while using the voting power of wet and dry states for huge economic gains for a select group of American legal and illegal businessmen, Wheeler got the votes he needed. The country was ruled legally dry. Dry was the green light for gangsters and their bought-and-paid-for politicians to continue to make money illegally with government protection.

President Harding's level of ignorance and lack of leadership left America vulnerable to smart businessmen and gangsters to become entrenched in American politics. Organized crime became glamorous. Greed became legal and was the new American Dream.

From the first day of Prohibition on January 17, 1920, to its last on December 5, 1933, America was thrown into internal chaos. The residue of an era that lasted for less than fifteen years probably supplied dirty money for many current billionaire American corporations. The contemporary government joke called "The War on Drugs" is the new Prohibition, to create another cadre of American billionaires legally through the illegal gangsters in the drug business.

Daniel Okrent, succinctly sums up the impact of Prohibition.

> And the 18th Amendment, ostensibly addressing the single subject of intoxicating beverages, would set off an avalanche of change areas as diverse as, international trade, speedboat design, tourism practices and English language. It would provoke the establishment of the first nationwide crime syndicate, the idea of home dinner parties, the deep engagement of women in political issues and the creation of Las Vegas. Prohibition

fundamentally changed the way we live.
("The Man Who Turned Off the Taps,"
The Smithsonian Magazine, May 2010)

However, change is dynamic; it sucks up and mixes all within its range. Little is left unaffected after the last domino falls. Consequently, the fallout from forcing the general public to modify their social and personal drinking choices led to an era where politicians, businessmen, and criminals became ensconced in a multimillion-dollar patchwork quilt of American greed and corruption. Gender and racial groups took on new roles. The new, emerging role of white women imprinting social change was forever changed, as well as that for the newly freed, fragile black population. Life in America changed for the better and for the worse.

Eventually, white women left their fingerprints and footprints on the legislation that led to the ratification of the Eighteenth Amendment to the Constitution on January 16, 1919. The manufacturing, sale, transporting, and importing of intoxicating liquors was prohibited in the United States and its territories. In the following year, 1920, women gained the right to vote. They had a winning trophy for each hand. It was a jubilant time and a new horizon for American white women. Unfortunately, Susan B. Anthony, the woman who was arrested for voting illegally in 1872 and was the architect for women's rights in America, had died sixteen years earlier. Susan missed seeing the birth of her lifelong passion come to a healthful fruition.

Flipping the Script

On the same time line, issues important to black women and their families were not so wonderful; the expectation for equality and fairness was not in sight. Although Harriet Tubman died in 1913 and had freed hundreds of slaves from the South, blacks were suffering under the harsh reality of earning a living in the industrialized Northern cities. The forty-six years between the abolition of slavery in 1873 to the year 1919 were filled with systemic hardships against black communities.

Although the road was not smooth, it was at least a paved street with a little optimism and streetlights. Black life blossomed in Harlem during Prohibition and was unlike many other places in black America. It was hard and poverty was pervasive, but at the same time there were a few pockets of the appearance of very good times. Harlem in the twenties and early thirties ran on two distinctly different black economic tracks. Although the few pockets of prosperity where the educated, professional, and celebrities lived seemed to rise above the daily struggles of the lower-paid workers, all of the black population received the same degree of disrespect and violence, brought on by a political climate of city thug and country redneck mentality.

The overall atmosphere of inequality for poor immigrants and blacks was only made worse by the ignorance of the rich gangsters, who were calling the shots in high places and local police jurisdictions. All Americans, in general, and urban black life specifically, would suffer during the era of gangster territorial wars and ethnic hate gangs. Bloodshed became part of modern-day American culture.

Unfortunately, organized crime and racism separated Americans again and placed them at odds in color and race wars played without rules. Terrorism and power became the tools of control. The war among foreigners in Europe had nothing on the war within America. The American appetite for superiority and control turned on itself as a battleground, and whites declared war on blacks and other vulnerable minorities.

The year 1919 began one of the bloodiest periods in America's history, and it was the precursor of the

Prohibition Act and the advent of the New Negro, returning from World War I.

Harlem's Black War Heroes and Their Music

On February 17, 1919, when their fighting in World War I was over, Lieutenant James Reese Europe returned to Harlem leading a victory parade up Fifth Avenue. Close to one million cheering black and white citizens turned out to welcome home the 369th Infantry, a war hero, and his new music. Ironically, this "victorious feat" accompanied one of the most single bloody years in American history.

Led by a hundred-member, mounted New York City police escort, they assembled in formation at Twenty-Third Street and marched uptown to a joyous reception, stepping proudly to music of James Reese Europe's Hell Fighters Band. The band was the first to receive recognition internationally as ambassadors of a new American cultural art, which was a new music concept expressing feelings and experiences of the Negro people. It was jazz.

When Lieutenant James Reese Europe of the 369th Infantry, leader of the Hell Fighters Band, played W. C. Handy's "Memphis Blues" in Paris during the Great War in Europe, Irvin Cobb, a war correspondent, indicated in articles that it was the best regiment band he had ever heard. While the Hell Fighters Band played at Tuilleries Gardens in conjunction with other great European bands, the large crowds (swelling to over fifty thousand) were eager to listen to Europe's music.

According to news reports, white European audiences caught a jazz-like fever and began to jump around wildly. Reese explained their jubilance as being a response caused by their unfamiliarity with hearing a different type of personal racial experience, expressed through music. Europeans were not accustomed to hearing Negro bands play. Lt. Europe's band interpreted the written music they played—that was not only in a syncopated manner, but the players were allowed, to some degree, the freedom to bring some of their own creative feelings into their playing.

The musicians improvised using the only experience they knew: their personal Negro voices. They played freely as they deviated from the written sheets. It was a new style of playing. Whatever the new style music was called, it drove the French audiences wild. At that time, unknown to both band members and audiences, they had experienced possibly the earliest sounds of a big jazz band. Jazz became real in France immediately and without explanation. They understood how it made them feel, and they were swinging and jumping for joy. It was the Hell Fighters Band that presented arrangements of blues, ragtime, and marches with such brilliance that other European military bands paled by comparison. The Negro music had put something foreign to their ears, and they liked it.

War Parade Heroes Strut to Jazz

New York City officials ordered the traffic on Fifth Avenue to be reversed, to flow uptown toward Harlem. Two reviewing stands at Sixty-First Street and Sixty-Second Street were set up for relatives and friends of affluent families. On the sidewalks, from time to time, police had to hold back throngs of flower- and flag-carrying wives and mothers, who wanted to embrace their returning heroes.

The NYC Board of Education ordered schools to excuse black students to see the parade. Whites waved from windows of mansions, and ordinary citizens lined the streets in one of the largest displays of unified praise for black men in the history of the city.

The accomplishments of the 369th Infantry was unparalleled. They survived 191 days under enemy fire, never lost a prisoner or a foot of ground they were to hold, and had heavy casualties. The 800 soldiers who remained in France under the command of Colonel William Hayward to receive the Croix de Guerre were chosen to lead the victorious Allied march to the Rhine. On that occasion, 171 officers and individuals received citations of bravery. This was a most unusual achievement for any regiment, white or black.

New Ideas for the New Music

Although the Harlem Heroes Parade was the high point of James Reese Europe's career, it is important to remember the positive impact he made on music before the war. In 1920 the New York Chapter of the American Federation of Musicians was closed to Negroes. Consequently, James R. Europe formed the Clef Club to serve Negro musicians as a network to negotiate jobs and to protect their interests. He regularly assigned bands to high-society parties. In 1911, a majority of the Clef Club Symphony Orchestra performed at the Manhattan Casino in Harlem.

First to Record

One year later, 1912, James R. Europe organized and led 105 men in an orchestra (with members who were excellent readers) in a concert of spirituals, plantation songs, choral, and ragtime, with ten grand pianos played as one at Carnegie Hall. It was a landmark event. Shortly thereafter, Europe became the first to record a black orchestra. It was Europe's ability to give dignity to Negro music, and to the general world audience, without compromising the honesty of the Negro experience. During that time, his music was considered new music by the audience. Most sources maintain the notion that supports James Europe as being perfectly placed in history at the right time, to skillfully connect the transition between ragtime and orchestral jazz of the future.

Recounts of his life from newspapers and magazines indicated he wanted to work on new ways to fuse jazz elements of ragtime with other forms to express the soul of Negroes, not imitations of what other musicians played. James Reese Europe's contributions were some of the most essential elements retained as jazz music matured and evolved at the onset of Prohibition.

Unfortunately, his plans for jazz evolution were cut short when after a brief confrontation, his drummer, Herbert Wright, stabbed him. They were in the dressing room of the Mechanics Hall during intermission of a celebration at Massachusetts State House, where they were appearing at the invitation of Governor Calvin Coolidge. Ironically, the battlefield war hero bled to death from a neck wound on a gig with his Hell Fighters Infantry Band.

What a Bloody Year

The year 1919 was the starting point of epidemic despair and violence, in the face of the possibility of progress. The year is significant because a huge door slammed shut and Pandora's box was flung open, flinging dangerous elements of unknown consequences into the atmosphere.

This eventful year is also often referred to as the beginning of the Jazz Era, the New Negro, and the Harlem Renaissance. Not all was as wonderful as it appeared; America's morality spiraled downward. Inflation was sky-high, workers were organizing and going on strike, immigration laws were excluding all applicants except those of Nordic or Teutonic bloodlines, and minorities were generally under attack nationwide. People of Jewish descent were being widely discriminated against and were often victims of violence. There was resurgence in membership roles of the Ku Klux Klan.

White Women's Pride and Joy Wore White Sheets

It is important to always keep in mind the political context in which historical events occur. While the women were desperate politically for support, many unforeseen bedfellows were made along the way to the delivery room to push out their baby, Prohibition.

It is crucial to understand that dry states, the Prohibition supporters, were numerous in the South. Within their ranks were the defeated Confederates faithful to General Robert E. Lee, who renamed themselves and formed the Ku Klux Klan organization to perpetuate their conservative, racist views for the America they envisioned, even though they lost the war.

The KKK organization embraced the ASL, anti-alcohol, Southern Christians, the Democratic Party, and xenophobia. The KKK was dry, Prohibition friendly, and in bed with the white women winners of 1919. Ironically, William J. Simmons, the Ku Klux Klan leader, was expelled as grand wizard because of, of all things, excessive drinking of alcohol. Simmons was replaced by Hiram M. Evans, who broadened the KKK scope of hatred to include foreign immigrants, Catholics, and Jews. During Prohibition, America's racial prejudices were out of control; New Jersey and Connecticut had larger Klan membership than Mississippi and Louisiana, and numbers were up nationwide.

The KKK, the Prohibition Party, the ASL, rural churches, and Wheeler were in bed together. The policy issue of dry state (anti-alcohol) and wet state (pro-alcohol) was the heart of the political power struggle of the 1920s.

Self-seeking, disgraceful alliances led to bloodshed in Williamson County, Illinois. Edwin E. Denison, a southern Illinois congressman, arranged for Roy Haynes of the Prohibition Bureau to deputize approximately thirteen hundred KKK members into a vigilante army, to clean up bootlegging. They were led by submachine gun-toting S. Glenn Young, who had been recently fired by the Prohibition Bureau and declared unfit for government service.

Under the cover of darkness, on the night of February 1, 1924, S. Glenn Young led the KKK vigilantes as they terrorized the homes of sleeping immigrants, primarily Italian families. Helpless women and children watched as the group slaughtered their husbands, sons, and fathers. Some males were dragged off to jail for having homemade dinner wine in their cupboards. The death toll by its end was twenty people killed by the deputized mob of Klansmen.

The Democratic Convention was being held in June 1924. Seeking some form of reprimand and justice, a resolution for the condemnation of the Ku Klux Klan was requested to be proposed. In defense of the

Williamson massacre, Methodist minister Reverend A. Stickney declared that only the Klan could protect America from Catholics and Jews. He added that the assassins of Lincoln, Garfield, and McKinley had been of Catholic origin. Nevertheless, confronted with countless accounts of atrocities, lynchings of blacks and Jews, and the fresh memory of the Williamson massacre of Italian immigrants, the Democrats did not pass the Klan Condemnation Resolution and left the Klan intact.

The Klan's stronghold was dry Christian states. Dry states fueled Prohibition. Prohibition was fast money—millions were been made from supplying the booze for the dry marketplace. The Klan used fear tactics to maintain the muscle needed to keep the political votes where they were needed to keep Prohibition profits in place in the South.

After the black migration to Northern cities, the census count remained untouched since before slavery, to protect the status quo. Therefore, Southern plantation owners continued to use the names of blacks from their property for a huge representation in political districts, to guarantee their high voting numbers. The Reapportionment Act was not passed until 1929. Millions of blacks living in "freedom" across America had been used as proxy voters for the interests of white Southern land owners for sixty-four years.

The calamities that were unleashed upon black people during the extremely racist 1920s era were summarily ignored by white America. The black experience was compounded by institutional racism and economic disparity. White women got the right to vote, drink, and smoke in public, and to socialize with black musicians and artists. Black people got to play their music and make recordings for minimal financial gain and for segregated audiences, but ultimately they had their rights stolen by white imitators.

Across the board, Prohibition gave America access to acts of violence.

CHAPTER TWO

"Prohibition Baby" Begets Gangster Culture

The country became embroiled in an internal, warlike police action, where the enforcement of the law absorbed bloody headlines in most popular newspapers and radio stations. Money and illegal booze flooded communities. Organized crime became a part of America's Roaring Twenties culture. The Volstead Act was the federal muscle set up to be the enforcers of the new law. Criminals became better armed to do battle with the new policing agents on the street. It was a dangerous time.

Prohibition gave rise to a lucrative industry called the bootleg trade, which in turn was governed by an executive division called "organized crime" to American society. America's new, wealthy, powerful, and politically influential organization, led by Al Capone, Dutch Shultz, Legs Diamond, and others, was needed to control the sale of illegal products in America. Many Americans had acquired a thirst for alcohol and continued to drink. Alcohol was supplied by a network of criminals who thrived on the inability of most people to legally make a purchase. In order to have an alcoholic beverage to serve at a dinner party or a wedding celebration, people would have to use illegal venders. Money of honest-working people, saloon drunks, and the super rich had to pass through the hands of the criminal network, if one wanted a drink. The bootlegging trade became a necessary entrepreneurial industry to keep American drinkers happy and the cash flowing. All phases of the process, from start to finish and up to distribution, was the virgin business territory where acquiring millionaire status was for the taking. Many businesses and politicians took plenty.

Local drinking holes began to spring up like a brushfire all over the country. Juke joints in wooden shacks, with tin roofs and dirt floors, flooded the rural countryside. Guitar-playing blues singers belted out sad stories of hard times and love. Old washboards and ceramic jugs—anything that made sounds—were used to make music. Spit-filled harmonicas, nestled between missing teeth, perched sideways across the wet lips of men who sang and moaned their blues away far into the night.

Women and men drank white lightning (clear white moonshine) and fully participated in whatever enjoyment they wished. They were out in the woods or on lonely, untraveled roads, where they operated out of the sight of Christian women. Local grandmothers and fathers became experts in the distillery business while their humble farms became crucial locations used as load-up points for bootlegger truck runners to big cities, to supply speakeasies and clubs.

Let the Good Times Flow

In downtown New York, the social life was full of places to drink and to see live entertainment. The very rich and not so rich all had places to spend money and have a good time. The 21 Club on West Fifty-Second Street was the most famous of all the downtown speakeasies, and it was one of the last ones to open in 1930. Owners Jack Kriendler and Charles Berns had other illegal spots in Greenwich Village: the Redhead, the Pancheon Club, the Grotto, and the Iron Gate at 42 West Forty-Ninth Street. Downtown speakeasies ran the gamut in terms of style and class, from the Stork Club and the Country Club down to the derelict dens of the Bowery bums.

There were clear choices for drinkers of every taste based on their ability to pay. Drinking created a subculture of its own. Geographic locations became key cultural markers, used to distinguish class and racial separations. Where one drank was more important than the quality of what one drank. Drinkers' inquires concerning content or place of origin of the liquor they heavily consumed was seldom an issue; the average drinking population did not seem to care. Most of the liquor was of poor quality and dangerous to one's health.

Speakeasy liquor was unlikely to be as poisonous as much of the saloon and the country juke joint stock could have been. In well-connected speaks in New York, some alcohol was distilled by professionals of bootlegging trade, who operated a tight control over the manufacture their product, with labels of country of origin. Unfortunately, it was also a common practice by some scrupulous bootleggers to manufacture labels and soak them in ocean water, to give the bottles an old, authentic look of an import. It was not unusual to find malt scotch diluted with embalming fluid.

British-imported whiskey gained prominence as an alternative to the Prohibition brands of questionable origins. The five British brands of choice were Johnnie Walker, Dewar's, Haig and Haig, White Horse, and Black and White. In many places, when an elite customer paid a dollar for an imported, reputable drink in a swank club, and a laborer ordered an unlabelled drink at a roadhouse for a dime, they would more than likely get the same drink.

To avoid suspicion, many cases containing illegal alcohol were shipped in boxes marked as floor varnish. Ironically the quality of the content was oftentimes not much better than the crooked, wet label. Bootlegging was a greedy business.

Gin became the perfect Prohibition drink. Women liked it, and it was easy to flavor industrial alcohol with juniper oil, glycerin, and water. The aging process in these situations only required the amount of time it took to get it out of the bathtub, into a bottle, and out of the bathroom. The raw booze was a great candidate for a sweet mixer flavor to hide the bad taste. The highball glass shape came into being to accommodate additional flavors and soda.

Bootlegger Joel D. Kerper was a major client for a Philadelphian industrial alcohol distiller. It was common practice to also use wood alcohol, isopropyl alcohol, and other toxic compounds. One condition, called Jake Leg, caused the drinkers to shuffle when trying to walk. The Jake Leg Walk, a crippling condition, was caused by untrained distillers adding a nerve-attacking dangerous toxin called tri-ortho-cresyl phosphate to their product. It was an unregulated market—there were no state liquor authorities, no tax stamps, and no legitimately regulated retail stores. No one was in charge of what was being poured. Drinkers did not care as long as they could get drunk. Police officials turned a blind eye to thirty-two thousand illegal drinking spots in the 1920s, which were always filled.

Jazz Music and Dancing Feet

For the most part, white women did not have to create a reason to frequent speakeasies with or without an escort. Many were set up like restaurants with servers, permitting the ladies to perch on stools and place their high-heeled shoes on the brass bar rails. Here they could eat, drink, and strike a pose to show off their legs to the men. The conditions for social and sexual integration attracted newcomers and young people. The emergence of dances like the shimmy and the Charleston accompanied open, freestyle sexual mingling in public. Men and women were awakening to new social freedoms.

Jazz music was new, as was the dance craze that came with it. Drinking in illegal places was new, and so was the illusion of racial mixing. The atmosphere of a carefree lifestyle set the stage for a successful run for jazz and speakeasy culture. Both needed room to grow and mature. Women were wild for the latest dance craze, the Charleston, which was set to music reflecting Scott Joplin's jazz style of syncopated tunes. Some dresses had long tops and short pleated skirts. Some were low cut, showing off cleavage. The hemlines always showed lots of leg. Beads, cigarette holders, and bright red lips were standard props. These women were referred to as flappers; sporting short haircuts and shiny headbands while waving their arms around wildly to fast-paced steps gave them an awkward, flapping appearance, like birds balancing on high heels and trying to take off. The men did the best they could to keep up with them. Many hours of practice went into the routine, with their hired domestic day workers.

In a May 24, 1925, article in the *New York Times*, "Charleston a Hit in Home, Dance and Ballroom," the author wrote,

> Proprietors of employment agencies are being importuned to supply cooks, waitresses, laundresses, and maids who can Charleston. The mistress humbles herself in her own domain and seeks with eagerness as a pupil the approval

of her social inferior. Broom and vacuum cleaner gather dust instead of routing it while the rug is turned back, the music machine is started and maid and matron, holding their skirts above their knees, go through evolutions of a modern version of a form of primeval jungle ritual. ... It is kind of buck and wing, of turkey trot and fox trot, a relative to all the dances of peculiarly Negro origin which have from time to time been modified and adapted to ballroom and stage.

Dancing to live jazz music became the rage for women, and so did smoking and drinking in public places. During early hours, white socialites and celebrities attended popular downtown speakeasies, where the well-heeled white clientele socialized. But after nightlife closed downtown, the party moved uptown to late-night entertainment venues.

Prohibition, Harlem Style

Nightlife in the early 1920s, just after Prohibition arrived in Harlem, was mostly tasteless burlesque. Harlem shows were more risqué than the raciest ones downtown. The Rockland Palace, formerly the Manhattan Casino, had shows where racially mixed gays and cross-dressing straights would perform in extravagant displays of clothing. The acceptance of open displays of gay talent was seemingly accepted in Harlem. However, these shows were quite tame in comparison to Mae Dix at the Little Apollo, located above the Harlem Opera House. The operator was Billy Minsky, and his comedy sketches focused on strippers. Mae Dix was the featured dancer, appearing in front of a topless chorus line, where she stripped down to just a banana between her legs. The Minsky Rosebuds had sold-out shows daily.

Dancer Isabelle Van would strip in phases. After several trips back and forth to the stage removing a piece after each exit, she would finally show one breast. Actor Alan Alda's father, Robert Alda, reportedly sang serenades between striptease and comedy acts. Minsky's market for burlesque eventually died out during Prohibition, because the audiences became younger, more educated whites who wanted to drink, dance, and socialize. Jazz music had gotten the attention of the night-time Harlem fun seekers.

Connie's Inn was located in the basement level uptown, at 132nd Street and Seventh Avenue. It was the popular first stop at the top of the partygoers' list, and it also had the highest price tag. The owners were two Jewish brothers from the Lower East Side. Connie and George Immerman opened the club in 1923, and it was named after Connie. It was mentioned frequently in the press that the club was opened to accommodate rich whites only, who were high rollers looking for drug-related and illegal Harlem activities. They had tables squeezed in so tightly that as many as 150 couples were able to see the live musical review. Fats Waller was joined by lyricist Andy Razaf to write "Honeysuckle Rose" and "What Did I Do to Be So Black and Blue" while working for the Immerman's. Connie's eventually became a "black and tan" establishment, by permitting very light-skinned blacks in for the late shows, to be seated away from the stage area. The shows had the benefit of exceptional musicians.

For those wanting more elbow room with a cheaper price tag, there was Smalls Paradise on Seventh Avenue, just below 135th Street. It carried a large crowd, and the price was right: the average check was half as much as Connie's. The bright lights of the long marquee extended out over the double entrance doors. Smalls was a bright, spectacular visual showpiece, an attention getter.

The Cotton Club, formally the Douglas Hall Dance Club, at Lenox Avenue and 142nd Street (the northeast corner), was originally owned by the black boxing champion Jack Johnson in 1920. A gangster, Owney "The Killer" Madden, bought the place from Jackson and opened it as the Cotton Club in 1923. It was rumored that Chicago gangster Al Capone was his financial backer. White writers from Tin Pan Alley wrote the Cotton Club Review material about the outstanding chorus line of very bright-complexioned, pretty Negro women. It was decorated to resemble an old Southern plantation with a wrap-around porch. The plantation décor was a comfort level for the elite customers—and it was a subtle reminder for the Negro performers to stay in their place.

High society was said to have preferred the Cotton Club. Paul Whiteman, Emily Vanderbilt, and West Coast movie magnate and owner of LA Chinese Theatre Sid Grauman were frequent guests of the manager, Herman Starks. Nightlife in Harlem carried an undercurrent of suspense and tension. The segregated, white-only clubs were located in a black community—however, the entertainers were almost exclusively black.

Lord, Please Let Me Hit the Number

Although many elder, local Harlem historians, including my Godfather Leroy Williams, indicated that Casper Holstein, an immigrant from St. Croix, was the creator of the Bolito numbers system. Holstein figured out the system from his experience studying clearinghouse totals, while working at a Wall Street brokerage house. Holstein's generous contributions to black colleges, Harlem's poor children, struggling artists, and museums came from his millions in the numbers business, but he did not make headlines or get the attention of a community of people impressed by sensationalism.

However, a black woman, Stephanie St. Clair, who came to America from Marseilles, France, in 1912, reportedly invested $10,000 in her own numbers operation Harlem in 1922 as a policy banker. St. Clair became a Harlem legend. Within a year she had forty number runners and made more than $500,000 with the muscle of hired men. Referred to as the queen of Bolito or Madame St. Clair, the woman ruled the Harlem area with extraordinary leadership skills and tough persuasion.

The hiring of Ellsworth Raymond Johnson of Charleston, South Carolina, was the beginning of a long criminal relationship between an abrasive woman boss and an ex-con pimp and stickup man who carried a knife and a gun at all times. Because of bumps on the back of his head, he was referred to as

Bumpy. Author Helen Lawrenson's book *Stranger at the Party* mentions that the violent nature of Bumpy Johnson's personality caused him to spend one-third of a ten-year prison term in solitary confinement for the protection of other prisoners. Queenie and Bumpy were able to hold off much of Owney Madden's grip on the Harlem policy game for many years, before bowing out under extreme pressure.

In 1923 when the Cotton Club opened with its new mobster owner, Madden controlled much of the illegal trade uptown. William Hewlett, his black henchman and an ex-World War I officer, was put in control of Madden's Harlem number concession. It made complete business sense to have a black man in charge of numbers in a community where 99 percent of the players were poor blacks. But Madden had to share the territory for years with Queenie and Bumpy.

Putting a black face to numbers gave a false sense of ownership to the Harlem community. The expensive suits and jewelry of Bumpy Johnson and Hewlett gave poor, hard-working people hope and the association of possibility of wealth, if they invested in the appearance of a local business venture. Numbers became their escape fantasy for a good future. The hopes of a nice place to live, pretty clothes, furniture, a radio, a piano, or a wristwatch motivated the devotion to their favorite numbers. They played addresses, birth and death dates, grocery totals, ticket numbers, and signs associated with dreams. Harlem residents took number playing as seriously as they took church, except that they did the numbers daily.

Numbers were a part of the wish list to make dreams come true in Harlem. The actual process of finding daily numbers was a science. Dream books were bibles for hitting the number. Every household had two or three copies. Anything that happened special with a number attached to it was played that day. Everyone knew their neighbors' and relatives' favorite numbers, and consequently people were also aware of who got paid off for a hit. A party or free food was expected from the winner or some monetary token for the losers.

Playing the numbers was the uptown version of the downtown country club. Every building and neighborhood faithfully paid money to their special, well-dressed runner, or policy collector. After collecting, he turned the numbers and money in to an area number banker (gangster), at the number hole. The runner was the daily social contact who knew all of their clients by address and name, as well as what they traditionally liked for the day. He was dependable and trustworthy. He was the intermediary between them and their money. Individual players did not deal with the banker, period.

In Harlem, waiting for the number to come on the block was a process. How it happened was a smooth-flowing, choreographed ritual. Everybody had their permanent positions. Many older women players sat in front of their buildings and on the stoop on pillows (to prevent piles caused by sitting on cold stone), and they tucked snuff into their jaw, dipped from small round boxes, and spit the juice into cans. Their thick legs were covered by a light blanket to prevent views from imaginary Peeping Toms. Others leaned out upstairs window, smoking and having coffee and then lunch, as they peered up and down the street. From time to time a string would be thrown down, anchored by a handkerchief or paper bag containing money, to a local truant kid to make a run to the store and then climb the four or five flights of stairs with the cigarettes or soda for a tip.

Only men—mostly unskilled and unemployed—sat on crates and broken chairs in small groups, on the corner or in vacant lots, sharing a bottle if one was available. Streetwise philosophy concerning legal, political, and sexual issues was readily dished out to the younger men of the village square. These consistent corner and street number gatherings became Harlem's cultural sensory pulse, garnered through the eyes and ears of the village.

Once the horses ran and the numbers came out, the runner would go back to the street and give the number of the day. Seldom would a winner be among the players. They would complain, recheck the dream book, look at a birth date, and put in their numbers again. The streets, stoops, and windows would be cleared out by early afternoon, only to start again the next day.

The runners and bankers made excellent money daily from the few dimes, quarters, and dollars from many faithful players. The occasional big winners were enough encouragement to keep the dream of future money alive for the rest. The gift of the Thanksgiving turkey from their banker made it feel like a family affair.

Numbers in Harlem was mostly a drug-free, cultural activity to share through the years with friends and neighbors. The game gave to Mister Hewlett power in a powerless, almost hopeless community of Southern migrants seeking a better life with a nickel and a dream. The power struggle between the two black men eventually had to play out.

Although Bumpy won a temporary victory over Hewlett (and the mob and Madden),and it seemed as though he had pushed Madame St. Clair forward as queen of Bolito in Harlem, the force of the mob was too deeply entrenched and organized in New York. They owned the police, politicians, and judges. The mob eventually won.

Bring in the Jazz

The Cotton Club was the ultimate toast of Harlem nightclubs, and it was strictly segregated for upper-crust whites. Mister Madden was known to be a big spender on his mostly black entertainers, boasting the highest paid in the business, and the most glamorous and famous clientele. Madden had the best shows in Harlem and introduced the songs "When My Sugar Walks down the Street," "Minnie the Moocher," "Life Is Just a Bowl of Cherries," "I've Got the World on a String," and "Stormy Weather." The club featured stars like Duke Ellington, Ethel Waters, Jimmie Lunceford, and Cab Calloway doing "Hi de hi de hi de ho" in a flamboyant, white, split-tailed zoot suit with a long chain swinging from his vest. Lena Horne was only sixteen when she was escorted by her mother to and from the club to dance in the chorus line.

The Cotton Club was more than just an entertainment venue. It offered a lasting contribution to Harlem by including jazz as a major entertainment staple. Irving Mills, a white music publisher, gained fame when he signed up and became manager of the young Edward Kennedy Ellington from Washington, DC. Mills kept Duke working as the chief band for the Cotton Club, though Duke played venues across the country and had worldwide tours for many years. Duke's nickname stuck because of his impeccable taste in clothes and his eloquent playing style and manner. He represented royalty. It was Duke who put the Cotton Club on the map as an exclusive club with a worldwide reputation. For five years, Duke was the Cotton Club's headliner band leader. Prohibition provided a big and steady paycheck for Duke and his band members.

The décor was frequently palm trees and foliage similar to the jungle flavor, with large leaves making huts around a few tables near the stage. The primitive mood and jungle-like themes frequently gave musical critics material for commentary concerning Duke's sounds as often being primitive; he was able to evoke moods of deep feelings from the band while the exotic solo dancers performed elaborate floor shows. The elaborate chorus line was overly stocked with pretty young girls. The qualifications were simple; to be considered, a young girl had to have very light skin; a pleasing nose and lips; long, shapely legs; a full head of very soft hair; and dancing ability. She would also have to have been born a Negro girl.

Ellington's musicianship was as impeccable as his lavish dressing style: cashmere coats draped over one shoulder, white flowing silk scarves, cigarette holder, and sporty shoes that set off his tux or tailored suit. His personal carriage spoke royalty. His originality, his volumes of great compositions, and the preciseness of his band made his performances fresh and popular. Duke symbolized not only the Jazz Era but advanced swing within the decade.

Duke lived on Edgecombe Avenue, in fashionable Sugar Hill in Harlem, and he created much of his music there. Dancers regularly danced the Charleston and fox trot to his orchestra's music at the Savoy Ballroom, near 140th Street at 596 Lenox Avenue. Duke was also known to hang out until the wee hours of the morning at a speakeasy, Mexico's, at 154 West 133rd Street on Swing Street.

The Savoy Ballroom was named after a famous hotel in London, England, the Savoy Hotel. Charles Buchanan, a black businessman, opened the Harlem ballroom in 1926. The Savoy Ballroom was the premier totally integrated dance hall in the country. The enormous glasslike, polished, maple wood dance floor had twin bandstands on each end. Movie star Lana Turner called the Savoy "the home of the happy feet," along with other Hollywood dancing friends like Greta Garbo and Marlene Dietrich.

The Savoy dance floor was called the Track because of the serious nature of the quality and amount of dancing done in an evening, with two great bands dueling. For ten cents a dancing girl would give a spin and a whirl. Dancers were called flyers because of the overhead flings and zips across the floor. All the big, important bands played there, but none was as popular as Fletcher Henderson's band, who was the all-time favorite.

Beign born in Georgia in 1897, just two years before Duke, he traveled to New York after completing Atlanta University to become a pharmacist. However, racism made it impossible to work as a chemist. In 1920, Henderson became a song promoter for William C. Handy. Inspired by Armstrong and Coleman Hawkins, he began to eventually get gigs where he could play in the swinging style. Rent parties and speakeasies were his favorite cutting sessions.

At a Savoy band battle, where the dancers were doing the lindy hop, jitter bug, and the stomp, got so hot some nights that the riot police squad was called to calm it down. The Track was fast and flying high. The quintessential jazz classic "Stompin' at the Savoy," by Edgar Sampson and Andy Razaf, sums up the fiery power of swing.

CHAPTER THREE

The New Negro Hidden under Her Skirt

The Prohibition Era served some people well. Except for white women gaining the right to vote, nothing changed for the worse for Southern white men. Their women were in liberation mode and were proactive on social issues, but the South remained constant and flew the Confederate flag to brand their plantation norms. Although defeated, the white Southerners thought he knew "his niggas" in slavery, but he had no clue of the "New Negro."

The relationship could and would never be the same again. The black soldier boys had used guns, fought and killed white men on the battlefield, and smelled victory. Their minds were forever open to the possibilities of complete freedom, and their hearts were ready to be brave in the face of adversity. It was a New Negro coming back to his family and country.

Imagine the ladies dressed in black in Ohio who simply wanted saloons to stop serving alcohol and to get the right to vote—they had no idea what was to be unleashed onto the world at a time that radical social and racial change was running rampant side by side with her dream of a successful Christian crusade. Quite innocently, her long skirts and petticoats had kicked up a trail of dirt along the complicated political trail that would eventually breed everlasting chaos in America. She was only doing what she thought was best for her family.

Timing is everything.

Stepping Out and Standing Up

James R. Europe, W. E. B. Du Bois, and the NAACP launched an intense anti -lynching campaign. Newspapers around the country in Negro city strongholds became advocates for the New Negro. The *Kansas City Call,* the *Harlem Crusader,* and *The Crisis Magazine* echoed it was time for the old Negro to go, and for the community to become more self-reliant and assertive. They didn't advocate violence, but they wanted to put an end to being on bent knees, pleading, and begging the white man. Negro intellectuals Alain Locke and James Weldon Johnson called for independent thinking and building institutional strength within the community. "Stand tall as a man," was the tone for the New Negro of the time.

Somewhere in the middle of this sordid patch of history, jazz was incubating within America's ailing womb. Jazz was still feeding to become a full-term, live birth, perfectly formed to symbolize all that had to come before in order to make it ready to be loved, claimed, and raised.

Jazz Fever Takes Over Blacks and Whites

Mississippi riverboats hired bands to play at different ports for people to come on board to dance and socialize. Southern gigs were few and far in between, and the pay was poor, but it gave musicians a chance to play together, a place to stay, food to eat, and the reward of a little traveling.

Through no fault of their own, on many occasions it was the first time that many of the small-town white patrons had ever seen Negroes in a close setting. Since the slavery economy was primarily concerned with Negro labor for the rural farmlands, white people living in small towns and cities had few, if any, occasions to see the millions of Negro people who had been attached to the massive Southern plantations.

Most white Americans had no idea what to expect of a Negro; they were functioning out of ignorance and myth. But all Negroes knew white people as either task masters in the fields, or from having worked in their homes caring for the children, sick, and elderly, cooking their meals, cleaning their homes and clothing, serving their parties, and adhering to their sexual demands. Between working in the white man's field and house, Negroes had hundreds of years to learn white Southern behavior. Now that Negroes functioned as quasi-free people, the learning curve for the white population was extremely disadvantaged. Black culture was unknown territory and a curiosity for the white riverboat social set.

Face-to-face racial social situations were virgin territory. Riverboat gigs were tense times for race musicians, as they were called, because the riverboats had to advertise that the band was not white; this was essential to control violent reactions to racial interfacing. Pre-warning gave the white customers a chance to decide whether they wanted to be in the presence of Negroes performing before they purchased a ticket.

Many canceled. Most were suspicious about Negroes wearing fancy clothes and neckties and shinny shoes and displaying stylish manners. The Negro members of the band did not look like the cartoon caricatures in newspapers that the whites expected to see. It was a new experience for small-town white people. Once the music started and their feet began to move to the music, it was unlike anything they had ever heard, and the band's race became unimportant. The music spoke to them, and they responded. Those who paid to come on board were never sorry.

St. Louis, Missouri, was the only port where the band had a chance to see other Negroes as paying customers. This port provided for both the Negro customers and band members the opportunity to interact. Coming on board to dance to their music was a treat. Negro dancers filled the dance floor with routines, fancy steps, and moves that the musicians understood and appreciated. The St. Louis port became a chance for the band to play the way they felt, and they held nothing back.

In 1919, while docked in St. Louis, Louis Armstrong jumped ship to celebrate his birthday. Local stories recall that Louis, Johnny Dodds, and Pops Foster went to a place called Boots Bar to buy a small bottle of whiskey. Louis heard that Prohibition was coming and wanted some whiskey to have on hand, in case they passed through a dry state.

These were lean times for young Armstrong, who was anxious to have a big career in music. He was able to work, but money was scarce and the salaries were low. To make extra money, Armstrong wrote original tunes that he sold to make ends meet. A music businessman, Clarence Williams, purchased a tune from Louis entitled "I Wish I Could Shimmy Like My Sister Kate" for fifty dollars. Louis was very pleased with his big sale and the good money. Not knowing the long-term wealth of the recording and music publishing business, he was happy to get what he thought at the moment was the large sale. The tune became a tremendous international success and bestseller throughout most of Prohibition, and it appeared in a movie. None of the financial benefits ever came to the naive Armstrong. Little did the three skilled Dixieland musicians know that the world was open, available, and ready for their raucous, foot-shaking style of music.

Jazz, which took its name from music
——Negro music——

Spread itself revealingly over the American temperament
And became the expression medium for it, a sign and symbol

Of the American pace, of its moving
spirit ...
—Charles Johnson, *Opportunity*, 1925

Jazz Finds Its Legs and Takes Off

The Jazz Era was to become the best of times for the
jazz musician to hone his craft in an intimate music
community of black masters. Harlem was the ground
floor of an American art form that would give to the
world an original American cultural contribution.
The demand for black jazz musicians to play in clubs,
cabarets, speakeasies, and dance halls in America
was never better. America's booming economy after
the war and the fast tempo of the spirit of prosperity
was unprecedented. Jazz fit the Roaring Twenties
mood of an optimistic nation.

Many white women blossomed into social butterflies.
Those with financial means quickly abandoned their
conservative, domesticated attitudes during the
lawless atmosphere of Prohibition. The climate for
new ideas, especially voting power, prompted women
to become more independent thinkers. There seemed
to have been a correlation between voting power and
a woman's lifestyle; she had a new attitude and a
new way of getting around town.

Driving an automobile added to the ease of mobility and independence of women of means. The Model T Ford, invented in 1908, was very popular, and by the 1920s the "Tin Lizzie" as it was referred to, proved to be popular. Many women included driving their friends around in automobiles as part of their new image.

The more independence a woman exerted, the more skin she revealed. Very short hemlines, showing lots of legs in smooth nylons capped off with high-heeled, fancy ankle-strapped shoes, became the rage. Bright fire-engine-red lipstick with matching fingernail polish, and circles of rosy rouge on perky cheeks framed by carefully sculptured flat waves of hair, served as a backdrop for peering doe eyes swept frequently by fluffy dark lashes. She adorned herself with miles of beads, cloche hats, furs, and tiny, artistically decorated purses dangling from long chains that hung from her hand or bare shoulder.

To set off the colorful, racy, flapper clothing fashions, the liberated woman's clothing was full of lines of fringe, swinging from her hips as she shimmed her way into a new sense of empowerment. The long black skirt, high neckline, tightly tied-down waistline, and thick cotton stockings of her liberators, upon whose shoulders she stood, were fading memories of the hard-won battles of the dark past. The passage of voting rights for women in 1920 was the turning point for American social behavior and political domestic policy. Women were excited by the idea of freedom, political equality to their men, and the ability to drink, smoke, and dance and go out at night, unattended, to places of their choice. Women were ready to kick up their heels, figuratively and literally. They were wound up and ready for ballrooms, cabarets, and speakeasies. Timing is everything.

A Bright Star Appears

On July 8, 1922, Louis Armstrong was in New Orleans, boarding a train bound for Chicago and leaving behind a salaried job of $1.50 a night. He was achieving a goal: he would be joining his idol, King Oliver. Leaving his hometown was not easy, but it was evident that traveling north to Chicago to make $52.25 a week plus tips gave the young cornet player an open door to new opportunity. Louis traveled light; he had one well-worn black tuxedo, his coronet, and a tasty fish sandwich from his mother, Mayann. At age twenty-one, Louie joined the King Joe Oliver's Creole Jazz Band at the Lincoln Gardens Café at Thirty-First Street and Cottage Grove. It was an extremely large and luxurious dance hall located near the stroll, the popular area in the heart of

Chicago's black South Side. Armstrong toured with Oliver for two years, gaining fame along the way. Louis was on his way.

Louis Armstrong's influence on the way jazz music proliferated around the world proved to be nothing less than monumental. His importance during the earliest incubation stage of the music cannot be explained in words, but his historical and everlasting influence on the people who consider themselves jazz musicians and students is unsurpassed. Fans called him Pops; royalty, heads of state, and international audiences referred to him as an ambassador. Louis Armstrong advanced the music upward.

Armstrong was a part of the Great Negro Migration, which lasted from 1917 to approximately 1930. He and over a million Negroes left the South for better opportunities. Entertainers, educators, skilled laborers, unskilled workers, and nannies moved to the North. The exodus swelled the Negro populations in Memphis, St. Louis, Kansas City, Chicago, Detroit, and New York, which in turn quickly created huge, urban black communities. All the migrants sought to fulfill a dream.

Negro women were a large part of the thousands that came to the North seeking jobs and a chance for advancement. The life of Madame C. J. Walker speaks to that quest. Although Madame Walker only lived fifty-one years, she made her mark as a millionaire in hair care products, and she left open the door for Negroes, and especially black women, to enter and thrive. As America's first female self-made millionaire—of any race—she set a great example for the New Negro of the Prohibition Era to step onto a better playing field than she had known.

Madame Walker, born Sarah Breedlove in 1867 in Delta, Louisiana, single-handedly broke the mold of the traditional black woman of the early 1900s. She kicked to the curb the black woman's assigned historical stereotype as the supportive, hard-working backbone and glue for the family. Sarah Breedlove, Madame C. J. Walker, became a million-dollar star in her own right, along with being a wife and mother. Sarah did it all. She expanded the world of possibilities to make something from nothing for all black women.

Walker's $250,000 home, Villa Lewaro in Irvington-on-the-Hudson, was built by New York's first black architect, Vetner Tandy, a founding member of the Alpha Phi Alpha fraternity. She died there on May 25, 1919. The year is significant because it is the same year of the historic, Harlem's Heroes Welcome Parade up Fifth Avenue. It was like two ships passing in the night.

CHAPTER FOUR

Black Women Sing the Blues

The human voice is the natural human musical instrument. Early on in the Jazz Era, women blues and church singers became performers in the American vocal arena. Rural blues and spirituals spread from church choir women who had strong voices full of emotional ability into revival tents of traveling evangelists. In small towns, especially in the South and the Midwest, ambitious preachers traveled a circuit, pitched tents, and preached about damnation, sin, and hell. They offered salvation or a blessed prayer cloth for a few coins. Strong female soloists were frequently featured.

Many early blues singers got valuable, on-the-job training and very little pay from these religious events. The leaky tent conditions were deplorable in hot summer and wet during spring rains, but people came to hear the singing and fire-and-brimstone preaching. Singers were guaranteed a receptive but critical audience and possibly the attention of a city vaudeville scout looking for a fresh face.

The rural juke joints, where customers drank and gambled, were frequently window dressing and acted as cover for the lucrative manufacturing of grain alcohol. Prohibition laws pushed the cash envelope forward for large numbers of rural juke joints and roadhouses to get involved in organized crime, through bootlegging illegal whiskey. Large sums of money from gangsters to set up distilleries and to ship cases of booze to cities was an opportunity for desolate locations to become valuable assets.

Negro women singing the blues in typical backwoods joints were used by ruthless owners as an additional drawing card for men to drink and spend their money. To attract young women singers, who wanted to get a chance for a better life, owners frequently promised good pay and connections to famous entertainers in big cities. Almost none of the singers received anything but empty promises. Juke-joint working conditions were appalling. Men who were drunk and abusive were tolerated. Seldom were the singers protected by the owners, who were primarily concerned with their sex appeal and willingness to tolerate the attention of drunkards, to pay for an illusion of a sultry sex experience through a hot song.

Singers often had their boyfriends to act as protection, and to collect owed salaries. Having muscle support in the early 1900s was the only way many black women could collect what was owed to them. However, everything had its price. The habit of using boyfriends, who were not talented or skilled in the music business, to act as intermediaries for black women blues singers between their paychecks and their work became a problematic business practice in the developing industry.

The road to vaudeville was a dangerous path for a woman to navigate alone. Traveling from city to city by bus or car and sleeping wherever possible was not safe. Performing where men dominated all aspects of the highly competitive entertainment business did not make being a poor black woman any easier.

Mamie

Talented singer Mamie Smith is credited with beginning the "Golden Era of Blues" and race records. Mamie's box office success opened the eyes of record companies to invest in recording black artists. Her sales pushed open the recording studio door. Mamie was also a part of the musical climate that framed the Jazz Era in Harlem. Mamie's unbelievable break came with a contract with Okeh Records; they released her recording of "Crazy Blues" in 1920, and it sold over a million copies in six months, as well as fifty thousand copies in one week in Harlem.

Mamie appeared at the New Lafayette Theater at 132nd Street and Seventh Avenue in Harlem to sold-out shows. The popularity of the phonograph—a new phenomenal machine that would produce the sound of music in people's homes as if they were actually present, just by placing a needle on a quickly rotating flat black disc—became the essential purchase for households. The record player was equal to the popularity of the family radio, but it was more desirous. It was a cheap way to be one on one with your favorite musician anytime a person desired. It offered control.

Smart manufacturers made inexpensive record players available for small-budget households. Having the technology to hear Mamie for fifty cents at home was a key factor in the overwhelming sale activity of her record, which kept her big wave afloat. The song may have been good, but it was the timing of technological invention that made her career take off nationwide for a brief time.

Ma Rainey

Gertrude "Ma" Rainey, born in 1886 in Columbus, Ohio, was looked up to and idolized by most musicians as the spiritual mother of the blues. Gertrude married Pa Rainey when she was eighteen, and the two of them traveled extensively with the Rabbit Foot Minstrels. In 1923 she was recorded with Lovei Austin's Blues Serenaders, and later she made "Dream Blues" on the Paramount label. A large number of recordings, made with some of the best jazz musicians available, followed. Louis Armstrong, Coleman Hawkins, and Tommy Ladnier played on some of her memorable hits.

Rainey retired at age forty-four to move to a comfortable home near her family in Rome, Georgia, where she died five years later. Ma Rainy was respected and loved by many in the industry.

Bessie's Tale

Bessie Smith was born in Chattanooga, Tennessee, in 1894; she was eight years younger than Ma Rainey. She listened to Rainey's recordings and fell in love with the blues. As a young teen, she traveled the South in a tent show with Ma Rainey, and she also followed Rainey to the Rabbit Foot Minstrels and Vaudeville

Blues. She got her break into the limelight when New Orleans pianist and composer Clarence Williams was searching for a rival recording competitor to match Mamie Smith's windfall success with "Crazy Blues." In 1923, when the recording of "Downhearted Blues" was released, Bessie Smith was proclaimed the empress of the blues. Bessie's career took off, and she was widely listened to by both blacks and whites.

Soon, recording companies such as Okeh, Paramount, and Columbia developed specialty labels exclusively for black talent. By isolating the market, the companies sold millions of race records. Bessie went on to record 160 recordings for Columbia and was accompanied by many outstanding jazz artists, who included Louis Armstrong, Coleman Hawkins, Fletcher Henderson, and James P. Johnson.

The empress of the blues became one of the most recorded blues singers, and she attracted the most loyal following of any blues singer. Eventually, Bessie Smith joined two other entertainers of the era, Broadway actresses and singers Ethel Waters and Florence Mills, to become hailed as the highest-paid race stars in the world.

Unfortunately, Bessie's glorious reign was for just a brief period. She lived the harsh life she sang about.

Her money and her first husband, Jack Gee, was not a good mix. Her violent temper and promiscuous love affairs with women and men kept the lyrics she wrote and sang about full of the pain her fans loved. At some point she formed a lasting and lifelong, common-law relationship with the uncle of Lionel Hampton, Richard Morgan. In 1929 Bessie made *The St. Louis Blues,* written by W. C. Handy. It was her only film.

On September 26, 1937, while traveling by car with Morgan, there was a terrible accident. Morgan misjudged his speed and rammed into a slower-moving truck in his path. Bessie's right side was crushed when he tried to maneuver away to avoid the truck. Dr. Hugh Smith and Henry Broughton were returning from a fishing trip and stopped to help. According to Dr. Smith's eyewitness account, Bessie's right arm was almost severed near the elbow and was losing blood. An ambulance was called for by Broughton from a nearby house on US Route 61 between Memphis, Tennessee, and Clarksdale, Mississippi.

During the twenty-five-minute wait, a new car driven too fast by a young couple plowed into Dr. Smith's car and into Bessie's Packard. At the time, Bessie was lying on the side of the road being administered to by Dr. Smith, and the ricocheting cars barely missed them.

According to the interview with Dr. Hugh Smith by Chris Albertson, Bessie's biographer, two ambulances arrived from Clarksdale, Mississippi, to accommodate a white and a black hospital. Immediately Bessie Smith was taken to Clarksdale G. T. Thomas Afro-American Hospital. She died later that morning without regaining consciousness after her right arm was surgically amputated.

John Hammond, Billie Holiday's mentor, gave a report to *Down Beat* magazine in November 1937 that has been the possible source of racists' rumors concerning the circumstances of Bessie Smith bleeding to death on a Southern highway. Hammond was not an eyewitness, and his story is wrong.

Unfortunately, Hammond's report of the ambulance drivers' refusal to take Bessie to a closer white hospital as being the cause of death is incorrect, according to an eyewitness present at the accident site. Hammond's popular and frequently repeated account is dramatic and typical of the segregation policies, but in this case the facts are somewhat distorted. Medical care was not withheld from Bessie Smith, and neither was she refused transportation or admission to a closer white hospital. Both ambulances arrived at the same time and were from the same small Mississippi town of Clarksdale.

True to form, Bessie Smith's husband, Jack Gee, twice pocketed all of the money contributed to place a stone at the grave site. Bessie Smith, empress of the blues, was buried in 1937 at Mount Lawn Cemetery near Sharon Hill, Pennsylvania, without a tombstone. To add insult to injury, it was a popular white singer, Janis Joplin, and a former childhood associate, Juanita Green—and not John Hammond, her mentor; or Columbia Records, with whom she sold millions of records; or her legal husband or lover—who placed a tombstone on her grave. It is inexcusable but true that for thirty three years after her death, Bessie Smith's grave remained unmarked. Two women stepped up and gave a deserving marker to a woman whose influence runs deep in the veins of singers worldwide.

Billie, Lady Day

Within the same American racial context, Eleanora Fagan Gough Harris, known as Billie Holiday, was born in Philadelphia in 1915. Eleanora's mother, Sadie, was a child of thirteen when she had Eleanora, and her father, Clarence Halliday, was only fourteen.

71

Sadie and Clarence married four years later and moved to a poor tenement in Baltimore, Maryland, to be near family members. However, the very young teen parents were unable to take care of themselves or maintain a stable home for their little girl. Clarence, who loved music, joined the army and was sent to Europe. By the time Sadie was seventeen, she was on her own to provide a home for her daughter.

At the end of his tour of duty, Clarence returned briefly to Baltimore for a visit. This was Clarence's last attempt at family life with his wife and child. Halliday moved on to pursue his music career; at some point he became a guitar player in the Fletcher Henderson Band.

At age ten, Sadie left her daughter with a girlfriend so that she could go to the hairdresser. While waiting for her mother, Eleanora was raped at the neighbor's house by Wilbur Rich. He was known to the family and had been in the neighborhood. Sadie reported the incident to the police and took her bleeding daughter to a doctor for care. The police arrested the rapist and took both of them to jail. The police subsequently placed the helpless, young Eleanora in a jail cell for two days as a material witness. The judge sentenced Wilbur Rich to jail for five years for rape. The court sent the violated and frightened ten-year-old Eleanora to the House of the Good Shepherd for Colored Girls for a few months, to receive adequate supervision.

While at the facility, music was played on the Victrola by the workers, and Billie fell in love with Bessie Smith's recording of "Down Hearted Blues." Bessie's sad lyrics became Eleanora's companion. Eleanora sang along with Bessie and used her own experiences of loneliness in her singing. Singing the blues with Bessie and listening to the horn of Louis Armstrong kept her company. Eleanora wished for a strong voice like Bessie.

Once released, her young mother, Sadie, did whatever she could to raise her daughter, whose body grew fast and matured with womanly features well before she was a teenager. She looked like a young woman instead of a young girl. By fifth grade, Eleanora the preadolescent grew tired of wanting nicely fitting clothes for her bulky body, wishing for lovely things she saw in stores, and hating her unkempt, "big-boned" appearance. There was little to like about herself or her life. She was tired of scrubbing the white slabs of marble stairs in front of the Baltimore brick row houses for a few pennies. She was tired of being poor. She wished her name to be Billie, like the movie star Billie Dove. She hated her life and school. She stopped going and started dreaming.

Two Girls in Need of a Mother

When Eleanora was twelve years old, she was tall and filled out as well as pretty, but her life did not improve. Sadie had little money or a place for herself or her daughter. Making ends meet became increasingly difficult for the young preteen and Sadie. Eleanora's household was in need of money. Eleanora became a sex worker at Alice Dean's waterfront whorehouse. She sang along with Bessie Smith recordings for tips at the bar.

Listening to Bessie and Louie Armstrong on the Victrola continued to be her private moments of happiness and training for her small voice, which she thought of as an instrumental sound. Her voice belonged to her, and so did her declining sense of self-esteem.

It stands to reason that her concept of male attention was shaped and constantly reinforced by neglect, sexual attacks by men and women while in jails, physical and verbal abuse, and fear of abandonment from an assortment of male figures. The men in her early life used her as a commodity for sensual pleasure while ignoring her need for kindness or affection as a young, developing teenager. Her female role model, her teen mother, was also a helpless victim and was unable to provide basic care for herself or her child.

Eleanora had a barren training ground for adulthood. She lacked the "home training" of normal standards. Very few life skills were available for her to draw upon to solve daily problems. For her protection she developed a sharp tongue and was capable of fiery bursts of temper. If she was offended, her communication style was reported to be raw and crude.

She was a prime candidate for male exploitation as she ascended the ladder from obscurity to fame, during one of the most socially permissive time periods in American history. Prohibition opened the gates wide for vices of all descriptions to flow freely. It was a new time and a dangerous time.

But timing is everything

Around 1929, the height of Prohibition, Eleanora's mother, Sadie, saved enough money working as a maid and part-time prostitute to move to New York with her teenage daughter. Sadie moved them into a nice apartment in Harlem, at 151 West 140th Street. It was a lovely building but was known to have a luxury bordello on the premises. Following her mother's lead, Eleanora began to prostitute for five dollars a trick; she was arrested and spent a hundred days on Welfare Island, just across the river from Manhattan. She said she was twenty-one instead of eighteen years old.

Eleanora finally took control of herself by renaming herself. She dropped Eleanora, kept a version of her father's last name, and used Billie Dove's first name to create Billie Holiday. She still was hoping to become part of the Halliday family in some form; however, the affection, love, and acceptance she desperately wanted from her young musician father never materialized. Rejection and surviving rape, jail, and abandonment was a heavy load for her young shoulders to carry. Billie Holiday became a self-made construct, formed out of necessity—the mother of all great inventions.

Having no more parental support in Harlem than she had in Baltimore, when she was released from the workhouse, the mature-looking teenager wandered in and out of small Harlem clubs seeking singing gigs. The numerous speakeasies on 133rd Street were perfect for her to experiment and to sharpen her talent.

Billie spent most of her time singing with house bands in Harlem speakeasies, where the best musicians in the world played on a regular basis. Billie was blessed to be coming into the business during the busy Jazz Era.

Although she was clearly not an overnight sensation, and sometimes she was fired repeatedly and then rehired because audiences wanted something bawdier, Billie continued to sing her style. Using a voice itself as an instrument for storytelling was too different for their ears. But she didn't give up her unusual style; she didn't own much, but her voice was hers.

The young Billie was confident she had something of value that was different and special. She was willing to learn. Billie had access to top-of-the-line black musicians at the Clam House, Tillie's Chicken Shack (previously Covan's), Basement Brownie's, Pod and Jerry's, and Mexico's for the musical skills and training she needed to become a great singer. Billie was a willing and dedicated student of the music.

In the Swing Street neighborhood, a popular and lovely cabaret singer, Monette Moore, was encouraged to open her own club in 1933. She took over the location of the former Tillie's Chicken Shack from the owner Covan, called the Morocco Club. When Monette took over from Covan, she named the place Monette's Supper Club. She welcomed the young singer Billie Holiday and her regular pianist, Dot Hill, to her new place as the house singer.

Within the flavor of the widely acclaimed poem from Carol Boston Weatherford, "Becoming Billie Holiday," lies the essence of how Monette's small act of kindness changed her life and history forever. Weatherford's text takes on the persona of Holiday in a very commanding way with such authority, until there is a willingness to trust the poetry to be authentic and in the actual words of Billie.

An excerpt from her poem, Too Marvelous for Words, relates the relevancy of the tale of the fate destiny had in store for the two women.

> At eighteen, I was hired to sing
> So the hostess could greet her guests.
> John Hammond, a young white guy
> Who dropped out of Yale to produce

records, had slummed uptown
to scout Monette, but he stumbled
upon me instead.
                              —C. B. Weatherford,
                    "Becoming Billie Holiday," 2008

The Discovery of a Legend in the Raw: Billie Holiday (at Bill's Place)

This particular Monette's Supper Club event is the single most important moment in time and accounts for all else to come in Billie's life as a jazz icon. It is also the most overlooked factor leading to her discovery.

According to commentary in Robert O'Meally's compelling book *Lady Day: The Many Faces of Billie Holiday*, John Hammond told Clarence (Billie's father) he had heard Billie sing at Monette's in 1933. Clarence indicated a cooler response to his daughter than Hammond expected, and he did not discuss Billie with Clarence after that brief encounter. Hammond had been genuinely impressed and worked to get her recorded, but no one was interested right away. Billie's voice and style was too different for commercial audiences, but Hammond continued acting as her publicist.

However, in 1933, Pod's and Jerry's at 168 West 133rd Street changed their name to the Log Cabin. It became a hot spot for jazz singer, song writers, producers, and promoters. Louis Armstrong's agent, Joe Glazer, came in one night to hear Holiday sing, and he signed her immediately. Glazer was also the agent for jazz singer Mildred Bailey and knew how to push singers forward. Billie Holiday finally had the help of professional representation.

Benny Goodman was at the Log Cabin one night, and he became interested in Billie. After Hammonds' introduction, Goodman agreed to have Billie record with his band at Columbia Studio on Broadway between Fifty-Seventh Street and Fifty-Eight Street on November 27, 1933. She recorded her first two songs, "Riffin' the Scotch" and "Your Mother's Son-in-Law." Columbia paid her thirty-five dollars for the session. Billie Holiday became one of the first black vocalists to integrate a recording session in jazz history.

Still, no one would record the young singer for another two years. In the interim, Billie worked at a regular Harlem gig at the Hotcha Club to make ends meet. Frank Schiffman heard about the new singer who seemed to be the talk of the town, and he was curious. After hearing Billie sing, he asked her to sing at the Apollo Theater for fifty dollars. She was thrilled but terrified of the notoriously critical Apollo audiences.

In 1935, it was the big night and she was petrified. Pig Meat Markham was the opening comedic actor, and he had to push her onstage to face the audience. Her rendition of "The Man I Love" brought the people of Harlem to their feet. Billie Holiday, age twenty, played to a standing ovation at the Apollo her first time out. It had been a hard, uphill, six-year journey from Swing Street, but she faced her fears and gained self-confidence.

Her father finally came to see her perform for the first time at her regular gig at the Hotcha Club, but he found nothing good to say about her singing. He did indicate that he felt she would never be able to support herself as a singer. Surprisingly, she was able to handle it because she never thought herself to have the strong, deep, rich, loud voice of Mamie or Bessie Smith. However, she knew she had something that grew from inside of her and that came from the common experiences of the blues.

Being associated with Count Bassie became the major turning point of her life as a professional jazz singer. Billie worked the 1930s and 1940s with the top jazz musicians in the business. Her career became lucrative, and she was able to support herself and Sadie in a grand style befitting her title, Lady Day.

In August of 1941, Billie eloped and married Jimmy Monroe, an extremely handsome, smooth-talking man with a questionable reputation. The twenty-six-year-old Billie, ignoring the advice of Sadie and Joe Glaser, married a man who loved women and opium. He and Billie began a drug-centered relationship of being high together, as though it were a special bonding for their love. The more they smoked, the better they got along—until the gigs dried up and Jimmy got arrested in California.

Before long the money and opium supply ran out, and Billie had to go home to Sadie. When she got back to New York, she found herself feverishly looking for someone to replace her husband as her opium supplier. A fellow musician, Joe Guy, inserted himself into Billie's life to be helpful with her drug addiction. Joe refused to deal in getting opium because of the telling smell; however, he introduced her to the benefits of a more clandestine product. It didn't smell, and it didn't create smoke. Heroine just made small needle tracks in the skin. Joe befriended Billie with an offer to take care of keeping her supplied.

Billie and Joe entered into a friendship driven by dependency.

Billie's mother, Sadie, died in 1944 while Billie was singing to a packed house at the palatial Howard Theater in Washington, DC, for an adoring audience. Billie was twenty-nine years old. Sadly, not even Joe's heroine was enough to ease the pain of her loss. The death of her mother left Billie devastated. Although her mother had not provided the best environment for her as a child, Sadie did the best she knew to do and always loved her. They'd had each other. Now there was no family who cared for her, or a family for her to love in return.

Depression and the increase in her drug and alcohol addiction put her on an endless treadmill of inevitable police trouble, man trouble, and gig trouble. Billie could not legitimately earn a living anymore or sustain her accustomed lifestyle. Her inability to even have a cabaret license—because of her arrest record, costly rehabilitation cures, and overly generous handouts of money—and finally the inability to entertain an audience on any level pushed her to her the lowest point of her career and life. Eventually, she was humbly accepting weddings and birthday parties to get cash. Major clubs serving alcohol could not hire her. Prohibition was over, and most speakeasies had dried up.

On December 6, 1957, Whitney Balliett and Nat Hentoff gathered a one-time-only live performance for CBS's *The Sound of Jazz*. Jo Jones, Count Basie, Thelonious Monk, Coleman Hawkins, Gerry Mulligan, Ben Webster, and Lester Young, her best friend, gathered there and recorded a legendary treasure.

Billie Holliday died July 17, 1959, after being placed under arrest and shackled in handcuffs to her metal hospital bed for drug possession, with a police guard at the door. Four months prior on March 15, when her close friend Lester Young had died alone in his room at the Alvin Hotel, she was denied entrance to his funeral. Her troubled life and career was like a phoenix.

Billie Holiday's name is one of the most recognizable names associated with jazz or blues, almost more than any other entertainer worldwide. Her attitude, style, and general visual and spiritual demeanor give her legacy as an icon from the Prohibition Jazz Era much staying power into the digital future.

Billie died at age forty-four. Her idol, Bessie Smith, was only forty-three when she'd died. Each lived extraordinarily close to the edge and ended life as sorrowfully as they sang.

CHAPTER FIVE

Swing Street

Many sources indicate that Billie Holiday was especially fond of the flavor of the music on Swing Street, which was a comfort zone for her as a young girl who hung out and worked as a singer. The street served as the safety net for jazz musicians.

The block of 133rd Street between Lenox and Seventh Avenues in Harlem served as an oasis in a dry, unfriendly, professional New York City marketplace for serious jazz musicians. It became the home for those at the top and those too broke to go anywhere else. It was the reliable testing ground for those in need of a start. It smelled of homebrew, pigs' feet, fried chicken, fish, and lots of smoke from of all blends of tobacco and weeds.

Harlem speakeasies became the site of late-night illegal drinking. The block had the highest concentration of speakeasies in New York. This block, Swing Street, represented a reasonably safe space for black and white people to come together for late-night and into early-morning entertainment. The rich and ordinary were treated the same and pressed elbows close together. Political and police activities maintained an unspoken hands-off policy toward their private, club-like existence. Organized crime paid officials well to develop a blind eye to speakeasy drinking and lucrative cash flow.

Speakeasies became the location for after-hours drinking in New York. When whites and tourists left Fifty-Second Street, they ventured up to Harlem. Speakeasies in Harlem were reasonably safe spaces. Political and police culpability gave a green light, which allowed a proliferation of small, privately owned buildings to convert their basements and parlors into havens for white society to come uptown for drinks and jazz after the traditional clubs closed. Black and white patrons were elbow to elbow with each other as they lingered into the early morning hours, intoxicated from booze and marijuana.

James Weldon Johnson remarked at length about his feelings for the relationship between the blacks, who lived in Harlem night and day, and the whites, who overran the streets by night. White nightlife and tourists came in droves by subway, taxi, and limousine to see how black people acted. They knew that Harlem had the unusual distinction of being protected by gangsters and City Hall.

Mayor Jimmy Walker, an extravagant dresser, was dubbed with the auspicious title "Night Time Mayor." Under his watchful eye, Harlem gained the premier position on the official tour must-see list. It was a nocturnal playground where everything considered illegal in other cities around the country was legal in Harlem.

Timing is everything.

A black artist for a national magazine in 1932, E. Simms Campbell, crafted a visual map of Harlem's coincidental double eras of Prohibition and the Renaissance, in the form of a pictorial map. Campbell's illustrated guide and map of the nightclub locations and notations of street interests for tourists gave fascinating information like the Crab Man and Reefer Man selling marijuana cigarettes two for twenty-five dollars, and stars indicated clubs remaining open all night. The scope of the territory covered was from Seventh and Lenox Avenues and from West 110th Street to West 142nd Street. Some speakeasy locations were omitted because there were too many to include on the map.

Regular, working-class black people were forced to tolerate some of their "loose-living neighbors," who used house parties to augment their low salaries to pay bills. Harlem was overpopulated, overpriced, and underserviced. Parents and grandparents attempting to raise and educate their children around loud-playing instruments, usually jazz musicians jamming the night away, struggled to maintain their Southern family lifestyle. The perceived picture presented was one of a happy tourist skipping and frolicking from one late-night spot to another, in a partying neighborhood that never slept. Harlem was a planned moral wasteland, created to keep the illegal activity away from the "decent families" of the white people, who came uptown to get the black exotic experience in a "look but don't touch" safety zone. It was the dark side of the new urban culture with a touch of danger, which was the erotic attraction of 133rd Street for white seekers. Rules of race relations and artistic form were made to be broken there, and they were.

Race Mixing

Along with the amusement-park mentality of the garish nightlife in cabarets on the main avenues and the numerous speakeasies on the side streets, local black women were uncomfortable with increasing racial mixing between white women and black men in Harlem. As it turns out, the majority of the jazz musicians uptown and the big-money local gangsters were black men. White women from downtown were curious and financially able to frequent the small, integrated speakeasies and attend the larger, segregated clubs whenever they wanted. Black male musicians were hired to play almost everywhere, and therefore white women had access to black male musicians in many social situations.

Blacks were not allowed to go to the major Harlem Clubs as customers, unless they were bright and looked white or were mob-related associations. Traditional, working-class men and women with families had few situations for social interaction with black professionals, celebrated artists, or entertainers. Family- and church-orientated single black women perceived drinking and drugs as unacceptable behavior for a prospective husband, and they held on to their Southern dating traditions.

However, the emboldened white female partnered with the "cool" black male jazz entertainers and celebrities, to the dismay of local women, and became a too-familiar, mixed racial arrangement for her to observe on her block. The mixed-couple dynamic model was crafted in part by the New Negro male. Thousands of returning veterans had served in Europe. The strict rules of Southern Jim Crow did not exist to the same degree, and many had experienced sexual experiences with white women for the first time. Foreign travel had permitted the black man to experience life as a man. He had tasted self-esteem as a human being of equal statue. His mental liberation as a new, free man enabled him to make choices of women from an enlarged pool of women.

The men came back to America during Prohibition (where integrated speakeasies in Harlem were prevalent) to exercise their opportunity to adhere to personal choices for mates. This was especially true for jazz musicians. Mixed couples almost exclusively meant a white woman with a black man.

The racial-mixing envelope was pushed hard and fast under the noses of black women by the popular celebrity Jack Johnson, the boxing legend and heavyweight champion of the world. For poor blacks and especially young black boys, he was a solitary symbol of black success. He was a black hero when there were none to look up to. Johnson was well traveled and wealthy, and he decided to invest money into a business ventured in the Harlem community. Johnson opened a nightclub, Club Delux, in 1920 and kept it three years. For unexplained reasons, in 1923 he suddenly sold it to a gangster, Owney Madden. With the support of Chicago crime bosses, Madden took over the club, changed the name to the Cotton Club, and initiated a whites-only segregation policy. It was not to admit black patrons, but it would hire blacks as help and entertainers only. Jack Johnson could no longer enter through the front door or sit at a table, but his wife could do so.

Prohibition's new mixed couple model was pushed to the extreme by Jack Johnson. He married three times, and all three wives were white. The first wife, Etta Terry Duryea, committed suicide after the first year. It was the same year he sold the Cotton Club and married Lucille Cameron, who divorced him in 1924. By 1925 he was married for the third time, to Irene Pineau. Johnson's preference for white women became an unspoken trend during this era, and it was highly disturbing to the white male population. Blacks had a love-hate relationship with Jack Johnson because of his refusal to have any personal relationships with black women except for the ones in his family. White men hated him for the same reasons.

Unconsciously or consciously, professional black men of financial and social status began to find a comfort zone with the idea of being around white women.

Unfortunately, the black man was positioning himself into a battle-like position against his natural mate, the black woman. Their common bond made during the trip from Africa across the Atlantic, down in the same rancid holes of the slave ships, was supposed to give her rights to him, or so she thought. Now that he was getting a small degree of status and a higher rank in the urban community, he appeared to forget that the extra food from the master's table and the small favors to keep their families alive oftentimes came from the black woman being sexually used against her will in the master's bed. Did he forget the price she paid for his inability to provide protection for her body or over their children's lives? Were her black attributes being viewed by him, her mate, as a sign of her inferiority, or was it simply because he felt the need to have freedom of individual choices, regardless of race?

America's segregationists were very persistent in trying to discourage and keep the black man away from his women. According to the Archives of the Tuskegee Institute, the total state-by-state statistic for blacks lynched from the first documentation in 1882 to 1964 was 3,445.

Between 1919 and end of Prohibition in 1933, there were 388 blacks murdered by white male mobs. Many of these murders were because of unsubstantiated complaints by a white woman against a black man or boy. Although lynchings were all too common during this period of American history, even in New York, in some states outside of the South the trend in mixed-race couples increased. Social familiarity and improved education of whites and blacks transcended the irrational color superiority standards of the white Southern Confederate mind-set.

But the fabulous Savoy Ballroom was another story. Everyone was welcome to dance together. Hard-working black men and women saved their money for tickets and filled the ballroom for a night of fun. It was a great way for blacks and whites to meet, dance, and mingle. All couples could take to dance floor, referred to as the Track, and dance the night away to big band sounds.

Life along Swing Street

Swing Street looked like a typical uptown block of narrow sidewalks and tightly bound side-by-side brownstones. Most of the buildings were long but very narrow. Usually the entering floor was where the parlor or sitting room was located for the piano. The kitchen, although small, was always turning out fried fish and chicken, pork dishes, pigs' feet, and barbecue combinations of all descriptions. The smell of skillets and kettles of food cooking didn't get started until after midnight, at about the same time the jazz would filter out to the narrow sidewalks. The block was drenched in smells coming from all directions, covering the block in a blanket of hot and spicy, ready-to-eat fried fish and chicken sandwiches wrapped in newspaper or on thick plates. The best smelling joint on the block came out of house 148, Tillie's Chicken Shack. It was clearly the best food on Swing Street.

Tillie Fripp personified the movie script of the young tourist coming to New York out of curiosity for a life in the big city. As a teenager working in an obscure roadhouse on Lincoln Highway in Philadelphia, she took her chances and traveled north to Harlem. But Tillie's life flipped the script and broke the stereotype. Tillie, a young black woman, became a success story.

It is the significance of the time and place that sets Tillie's story in the most extraordinary set of circumstances. Since the abolition of slavery, at no other time in American history have two roads crossed in New York City where the results would change the manner in which blacks and whites socialized.

Tillie came to town just in time for the onset of Prohibition's dirty underwear to star to show up with organized crime and the arrogance of the Harlem Renaissance (the New Negro and white women). With that powerhouse duo, the toothpaste was out of the tube and would never go back in.

These two intertwined, significant historical eras, Prohibition and the New Negro, created the cultural context and directly influenced Tillie's destiny. Within the belly of this strangely conceived era were cross-germinated twins. The white woman got the right to vote, and the black man decided to stand upright and no longer be a boy; it caused them to mix about in a newly written script. Each was exploring a new role that had no previous American constitutional format.

As the story of another script goes, the young girl Tillie left her job at a Philadelphia roadhouse with two weeks' pay, with the intention of coming to New York to see what big-city life was all about. While visiting a club with a friend, she was approached by a speakeasy owner in need of someone to serve dinner to his customers. He offered Tillie free rent and the use of a stove; however, she would have to pay for gas, have her own utensils, and serve the dinners. She used all she had and could borrow, and with $1.98 she accepted the deal, knowing that her roadhouse job would always be there if things did not work out.

Tillie shopped, cooked, washed dishes, served, and greeted her boss's speakeasy customers with fried chicken, biscuits, and ham and eggs. Although fried chicken was her specialty, it was a combination dish that was a hit. A newspaperman passed on to Louis Sobol, a writer for a popular downtown New York paper, the scoop on Tillie's cooking mastery of a dish coined "porker-crackle-berry combination."

Louis Sobol became her guardian angel. Sobol was a highly respected Broadway columnist for the Hearst newspapers for over four decades, the *New York Journal* and *Journal American*. His influence in high society was from writing the byline "New York Cavalcade," a chronicle of show business when Broadway was the center of the entertainment world. Louis loved her cooking and made sure his well-heeled friends showed up to support his newfound Harlem interest. Tillie's reputation grew faster than she was able to produce food.

Tillie Fripp was a one-woman show. She proved to be a genius in public relations and developed an enduring personal style with her customers, which held them faithful and tolerant as she rushed them off their stools and out the door, to make room for the next ones on line. Before long, her followers were lined up outside her narrow doorway, off the sidewalk. Customers lined up to get in to Tillie's. The celebrities waiting in their automobiles for special treatment to go the front of the line were forced to share the sidewalk with those going to the Clam House.

The clientele attracted to the Clam House enjoyed the risqué nature of the sexually diverse and nontraditional entertainment. The space of the side-by-side speaks and clubs was very narrow. Those waiting outside had plenty of time to enjoy the street's flavor and the diversity of the block, just by being present in Tillie's line. It's not unreasonable to assume that many people passed up the food and went to see the live show next door. The strip was a perfect conduit for traffic sharing; it was great overflow activity for Tillie's small, new business.

Quickly her boss felt overshadowed because Tillie was earning more money than his speakeasy. Because of the caliber of her upscale Broadway clientele, her customers refused to buy the speakeasy's low-quality gin and questionable moonshine whiskey with barely dry labels. After a serious quarrel with her boss concerning her refusal to sell his alcohol to her dinner customers, Tillie more than likely felt she had no choice but to quit or ignore the wishes of her customers. She knew she was on to something bigger than being his cook and server. There were very high stakes riding on her next move. Although she was grateful to him for accepting her without any experience working in New York and giving her an opportunity to discover her talent, she wanted to make her own decisions.

After what must have been a lot of floor pacing and praying, Tillie decided to quit her reliable job. She collected her utensils and moved next door, into 148. There she opened her own place and called it Tillie's Chicken Shack. She was officially in business on Jungle Alley. It was on the ground floor of a four-story brick building, and she was her own boss to do as she pleased. She took a chance on herself and Harlem.

Timing Is Everything

Scared but determined, this black woman took her newborn business quickly to full adulthood in a time that Madame C. J. Walker, the first American millionaire, was the only black businesswoman in Harlem to emulate. In just three years, Tillie developed a following of celebrities and personalities that rivaled all the major clubs. Her reputation spread across the country because of the tales her white customers told wherever they traveled.

According to the *New York Age* newspaper, columnist Lou Layne had a byline of "Moon over Harlem" and stated,

> Downtown columnists like Louis Sobol laundered her with praises and before long Fripp had enough capital to open her own restaurant at 148 West 133 Street. Tillie's chicken and waffles became musts for every in-the-know tourist, and her menu was augmented with a jazz line up that came close to matching the Nest in quality and variety. The success of Tillie's and the Nest led to more clubs on what had formerly been a genteel residential street.

Swing Street Was Jumping

Tillie was a major attraction on the busy block, and clubs and speakeasies surrounded her establishment on both sides. On October 19, 1928, next door to the east of Tillie, Edith's Clam House at number 150 opened with Gladys Bentley. Bentley was a garish female impersonator who wore a top hat and tuxedo tails. Much of her musical material was sexually provocative and X-rated.

On the opposite side of Tillie's Chicken Shack, going west, was Brownie's Basement at West 152, and in another basement-level club was Mexico's at West 154. Mexico's was Duke Ellington's favorite, and it was a draw to the block for a huge following of jazz musicians for cutting sessions. Young musicians felt privileged to have their chops put on the block by the seasoned veterans of the jazz world, who spent hours sweating out their souls in a safe space.

Several doors down from Duke's late-night hangout was the Log Cabin, also known as Pod's, at 168 on the ground floor of a gorgeous brownstone. The owners, Jerry Preston and Charles Hollingsworth, placed a triangular-type structure over the entrance and covered it with logs. Directly across the street was the Nest at West 169, and it was the premier club of all of 133rd Street.

Not only was the Nest the biggest and most lavish, but its owner, John Carey, pulled the best entertainment and big spenders. Swing Street was hot with good food, blues singers, and live jazz. Times for the blacks involved in the entertainment and club life were making money.

Tillie made huge amounts of money quickly. Many of Tillie's white patrons came from Connie's Inn customers, who, after tiring themselves out dancing the lindy hop and the Charleston, walked one block around the corner to her all-night speakeasy to continue drinking and eating Southern-style fried food. There, everyone mingled as racial equals. However, very few local black women made the street and speakeasies their choice for socializing. For the most part black women went to cheaper rent parties, where they could easily socialize with the black musicians and enjoy the jazz music.

The small, dimly lit, smoke-filled, overcrowded spaces made the mystic of the urban subterranean clubs exciting. It was fashionable to drink the alcohol from plain teacups instead of glasses, to keep the occasional eye of the police officers away from the crime. The upright pianos in most of the small, cozy speakeasies were poorly tuned, but no one cared. The powerful left hand of the piano players kept the stride tempo flowing regardless of the situation.

All of the musicians were free to play for their own satisfaction and with other comparable talents whom they respected. They had fun and formed relationships based on mutual admiration. They almost always drank too much. Before the sun came up, it was hard to predict who would to drop by to sit in and jam. These were the magic moments that kept the white and black attendance high. Black jazz giants were very much in the house.

Swing Street was a breeding ground for conventional and social rules to be reshaped. Writers, actors, dancers, and musicians came together without a need to define race or gender, and to enjoy intimate, face-to-face relationships orchestrated by jazz masters working just inches away. It was music up close and personal, the way jazz happens in the moment of unexplained, collaborative energy. Jazz was creating a home for itself on Swing Street.

Young musicians had the rare opportunity to show up and perform with some of the greatest musicians of the era. Willie "The Lion" Smith and Garland Wilson's strong, upbeat tempo to their piano styles attracted many talents. It is rumored that Fats Waller played one song twenty-eight different ways to win a free drink for each song change. He won the bet, but no one is sure how many he drank. Fats was aware of his love affair with liquor. To make sure he could drink until satisfied and sleep as long as possible between gigs, he secured a nearby place on Swing Street to go sleep it off. Waller made many trips to 107 West 133rd Street to Mother Shepherd's Speakeasy and Boarding House.

Excessive smoking and drinking gin were typical behaviors displayed in late-night joints, but these were just the tip of the iceberg. Interracial couples evolved over time. Constant exposure of black male jazz musicians and white female customers set into motion opportunities to become curious about the possibility of interracial, intimate relationships.

The exotic nature of the close proximity of race and gender added excitement to the new speakeasy fad for the newly liberated white woman. She could not only observe the mythical black man and his culture openly, but she could make her own decisions, as she had always done, about what to do or not do about it. But leaving things as they were originally had not been her nature.

Tillie very quickly needed more space, and she had become a celebrity in her own right. A local businessman, Covan, bought Tillie's place. Not only did Covan take over from Tillie, but he negotiated a deal in which Tillie was to leave the name with the location, because the location had become a drawing card on the block. The official name, Tillie's Chicken Shack, remained at the 148 location, allowing the fame of Tillie's Chicken Shack to continue intact— and most of all, allowing Covan to receive the positive financial fallout from Tillie's popular coattails. When Tillie moved farther down Swing Street to Lenox Avenue at 133rd Street to a larger place, it was called Tillie's Chicken Grill. After the sale to Covan, she did not use her original name again, but neither did she need it. Her reputation was beyond a single location; she was a brand.

In 1935, the boxer Jack Johnson opened a new restaurant on the West Side in the midtown Tenderloin district, and it attracted a stellar crowd. Tillie Fripp opened her new restaurant on Forty-Ninth Street and gave Johnson stiff competition. Tillie employed over twenty Harlemites, a bookkeeper, and a chauffeur; she established herself as a hardworking, independent businesswoman. Her associations were as diverse as her menu had become over the years.

Tillie's new experience as a businesswoman was the beginning of a new attitude and lifestyle that had become popularized by the new wave of heightened self-respect among blacks in New York. Based on their experiences in Europe during the war and the slight improvements in living conditions with paychecks, blacks began to have higher expectations for a better life, although the reality of a "better life" was not evident in Harlem generally. The depressed economy laid a heavy burden upon optimistic poor people.

Changes in the Swing

The New Negro was a post-slavery construct by the intellectual scholars and writers of the Harlem Renaissance era. The New Negro was expected to step away from the old and leave it behind, in exchange for a new consciousness of independence, self-sufficiency, militancy, and self-assertion of increased worth and value by Western society. The New Negro was an intellectual and social construct, and he stepped away from the past.

W. E. B. Du Bois, following on the heels of Alain Locke as pioneer Harvard graduates, emerged as the militant intellectual integrationist to shape the attitudes and actions of his people. Du Bois, unlike his predecessor Booker T. Washington, believed intellectualism would transform society from segregation to homogenization through the acceptance of the Talented Tenth. Du Bois felt that interaction between bright black professional writers, doctors, lawyers, composers, and teachers, and white movers and shakers, would create a common ground for communication. A cultured New Negro was essential for the Du Bois paradigm.

In contrast, jazz composers and musicians accepted new and old Negro culture. They lived with the new, free, and open spirit, but their music remained true to the old, historical, traditional slavery core. Their music dug deep to hold on to their African roots of rhythm to link together the field hollers of the plantations, as well as the pain and humiliation of the auction block, to fuel the fire of artistic expressions through their music. Jazz music had a personal fingerprint of the American slave experience and the daily degradation of racism as an unfortunate birthright that belonged to the old and new black American.

It was this strange fruit that was born through jazz. By virtue of its components, the origin of jazz has its unique American, noble black crest that separates and distinguishes it from all others. Jazz is grounded by its roots. Both the Jazz Era and the Renaissance's New Negro concept ran concurrently. They were intrinsically intertwined with a common history but separated by artistic perceptions.

Nathan Irvin Huggins, author of *Harlem Renaissance*, made a keen observation of what I perceive as the basic dissonance between the New Negro and Jazz Era music. Huggins notes that

> In a very vital and real way, that folk culture and tradition was undergoing the genuine alchemy of art. Work songs, gospels, and hollers were being transformed into blues, ragtime, and jazz. But, strangely, although black intellectuals were quick to acknowledge the contribution of black music to America culture—the only distinctive American contribution as it is often put—they are rarely willing to claim it was serious music of high culture.

> And while many Harlem intellectual enjoyed the music of cabarets, none were prepared to give someone like Jelly Roll Morton the serious attention he deserved. Jazz was infectious entertainment and not an ingredient of high civilization. So, provincialism pulled the black intellectual— like his white American brother—away from the culture of his experience into the culture of his learning.

Superior black jazz musicians flooded Swing Street from corner to corner after they finished gigs downtown. Piano player William Henry Joseph Bonaparte Bertholoff Smith, known as the Lion, said he earned his nickname for bravery in battle in World War 1. At other times he claims he was named "the lion of Judea" because of his devotion to Judaism. The stories worked for him.

The Lion was a great friend and rival of James P. Johnson, pianist, conductor, arranger, and the unquestioned elder musical statesman; Johnson's piano rolls inspired Duke's musicianship. Johnson was a large man who was known to enjoy large cigars. He was a quiet, shy man who lived in a house in Queens with his wife. However, he loved coming to Harlem to be near live jazz, and to duel with the Lion and Duke. They played duels regularly and for long periods of time. On a few occasions, Johnson's wife would go up and down Swing Street or other blocks, listening to the pianos being played. When she recognized his special stride style, she would follow her ear to the proper apartment or speakeasy, go in, and firmly usher him back home to Queens. Johnson did not resist.

Duke always referred to Willie as the Lion. Willie continued the fierce dueling piano ritual until Duke had had enough and decided he wanted to devote more time to writing original music. Their carving battles, as Willie called them, sometimes lasted four or five hours. Duke's favorite after-hours speakeasy was Mexico's at 154, near the middle of the block.

Around the corner and farther up Lenox Avenue, Mills managed to keep Duke's orchestra working as the chief act at the Cotton Club at 142nd Street for five years in Harlem. Duke's international success never allowed him to be free to spend uninterrupted time in Harlem or anyplace else ever again. However, he did get a chance to occasionally go back to his gin joint.

In a 1930 article from the *Amsterdam News,* Irving Mills, Duke's music publisher, stated, "The Negro is the rightful exponent of jazz, and its development and exploitation has been the basis on which all white musicians have built their experiments."

According to personal accounts, private sources, and printed materials like the article, The Rise and Fall of The Original Swing Street, by David Freedland, November, 16th-22nd issue in 2005 of the *New York Press*, mentioned speakeasies which were plentiful on the West 133rd Street block. Making a casual stroll down the celebrated block offers a rare opportunity to see some of the actual locations where unusual relationships were formed around jazz and drinking. The uniqueness of the interracial and cross-cultural exchanges which were experienced on the block, have long since given up its ghosts.

Except for one speakeasy at number 148, Bill's Place, all others are silenced by the wrecking ball, converted to private homes or churches, or remain looming like abandoned memories that will not die.

CHAPTER SIX

Revisiting the Past

Take a walk going south from 135th Street on Lenox and Malcolm X, and make a right turn onto 133rd (Swing Street), home of the speakeasies and buffet flats. Refer to the map insert for the scene in 1932, but for now follow the addresses from east to west to Seventh Avenue and Adam Clayton Powell Jr. Boulevard.

Here are some location sites of former Swing Street Speakeasies that were active during the Prohibition Era of the 1920s and 1930s, along with pictures of what has become of the sites as of 2013.

At **107** was **Mother Shepherd's Speakeasy and Rooming House**. This was the place where Fats Waller stayed when he needed to sleep it off.

At **146** was the former location of **Edith's Clam House**. The Clam House had the distinction of having sexual, X-rated shows of mixed gender and straight performers.

Next door was **148** (now Bill's Place), the location of the critically acclaimed food of **Tillie's Chicken Shack**. Owner Tillie Fripp, from Philadelphia, was not only a talented cook, but she was smart enough to cash in on her popularity and buy the four-story brick building. Her famous chicken, ham, and eggs became her road to success. Because of the NYC press attention, her speakeasy attracted key performers like Willie "The Lion" Smith, Fats Waller, James P. Johnson, and Billie Holiday.

At **152** was **Brownie's Basement.** Very little was recorded about this speakeasy.

Number **154** contained **Mexico's,** Duke Ellington's favorite gin joint on Swing Street. Duke enjoyed the company of very distinguished white guests, who followed him from the Cotton Club to his gin joint. There his fans could mix racially and interact equally. They'd hear great musicians who came to be in young musicians' company during the late hours and drink fresh bathtub gin from teacups.

At number **168, the Log Cabin (the Pod)** speakeasy was owned by Jerry Preston, a well-to-do gambler, and his partner, Charles Hollingsworth. The décor was luxurious and hosted a faithful upper-class clientele.

The Nest at **169** was one of the first major speakeasies to open on Swing Street, on October 18, 1923, by owners Mal Frazier and John Carey. The Nest was on the north side of 133rd Street, close to Seventh Avenue (Adam Clayton Powell Jr. Boulevard), and in an independent, freestanding, two-story building with a full basement. Chandeliers, draperies, and expensive appointments made the Nest a showcase. The Nest had a large dance floor surrounded by tables. The entertainment was more formal than that of the traditional small speakeasies on the south side of the street. Mal and John had the most popular and spacious speak on the street. The Nest survived the depression and the repeal of Prohibition, and it remained open into the late 1930s.

When Nest co-owner Mal Frazier allegedly stole a large amount of money from the Cotton Club owner, Owney Madden, a known mobster with ties to organized crime, the business went downhill. The confrontation was said to have been ugly. The police became involved, and the popular Swing Street jewel came to a gradual end. Luckily, no one was killed.

The Nest building, at 169 West 133rd Street, was bought and sold to different club owners. The building stayed in business longer than any of the other speakeasies on the block before it closed in the 1980s. The abandoned structure still stands as a forgotten testimonial to the reality of Swing Street, and it is slated to be demolished in 2013.

107 West 133rd Street,
Mother Shepherd's Speakeasy and
Rooming House

146 West 133rd Street, Edith's Clam House

148 West 133rd Street, Tillie's Kitchen Shack

152 West 133rd Street, Brownie's Basement

154 West 133rd Street, Mexico's

168 West 133rd Street, the Log Cabin (the Pod)

169 West 133rd Street, the Nest

169 West 133rd Street, the Nest

CHAPTER SEVEN

Harlem's Dirty Linen

On December 5, 1933, the repeal of the Eighteenth Amendment brought the close of a short era that changed American culture and eventually the world's exposure and acceptance of jazz music as an art form of American blacks. Although the political era came to a halt, and the numerous private cabarets, speakeasies, and gin mills dried up, Prohibition created Swing Street on West 133rd Street between Lenox and Seventh Avenues. The block gave rise to speakeasies, and from those small havens, the great jazz musicians came to fruition; in turn they produced for the world a more refined, original American art form, jazz. But that's about it. The Jazz Era is the only lasting cultural product of value that Prohibition can be proud of nurturing in Harlem.

Nonetheless, unsubstantiated stories as enchanting as children's fairytales persist relating to Prohibition and even the Harlem Renaissance. For some reason there are sporadic calls for going back to "the good old days" or "back in the day," when things were wonderful. Why go back to something that held more mystique than substance, especially for the black working people in the community? Please, no more calls to rejuvenate the romantic notion of attaching the current gentrification changes needed to a mythical theme, "The Second Harlem Renaissance." This is an overblown fantasy.

Peeling back the curtain of time covering the well-staged piece of American urban nostalgia for a broader view gives life to a reality show lived by real people in the Harlem community. Generally speaking, all the intense activity that erupted in the small geographic area called Harlem was a bit too much trauma for any struggling community to digest and remain healthy.

The original Harlem Renaissance was conceptually elitist by the nature of its design, when it was recognized in 1924 at a dinner at the Manhattan Civic Club. It has been said that it was this occasion, sponsored by *Opportunity Magazine,* that gave formal recognition to black writers before an affluent black and white audience. But it also offered an alternative mindset needed, for an overall intellectual boost for heightened black consciousness. Du Bois, Locke,

McKay, Toomer, Fauset, and Hughes were among the guests for the next several years of the annual event.

A few of the egalitarian writers and artists did receive financial and professional gain, along with dual memberships between the two Bohemias, black Harlem and white Greenwich Village downtown. Those who had the attention and financial favors of wealthy white benefactors like Charlotte Osgood Mason rose to fame and national prominence. The chosen few New Negroes were savvy enough to accept financial support and somehow remain faithful to their black roots. They took advantage of advanced studies in universities, especially Columbia University in Harlem, as well as international travel. Some had their manuscripts published.

Osgood's devotion to primitive arts and their artists was a popular white philanthropic phase, which benefited many New Negro intellectuals who were in need of support during the heyday of Harlem's emerging, small, black, college-educated, middle social class. Zora Neal Hurston, among others, benefited greatly from her support. The extremely wealthy Charlotte Osgood, referred to as Godmother, was known for using her lovely downtown Park Avenue apartment and for gatherings of black writers to read from their works, depicting the Negro experience and spending long periods of time discussing Negro issues to entertain her friends. She was reported to have given cars and regular stipends to ease the annoyance of her insistence on directing their work to use language of ignorant, uneducated blacks in their works. Hurston's work reflects the Park Avenue dowager's influence for primitive language patterns that confirmed white perceptions of the black population's lack of proper English usage. Zora received her master's degree and eventually moved south after flooding the publishing market with black rural dialect.

The café society class of white women enjoyed small afternoon luncheons where they could drink bootleggers' illegal booze and gin cocktails, smoke cigarettes, and engage in culturally enlightening conversations with invited guests. Educated Negroes who were well spoken succeeded in capturing their attention and served as their objects of ethnic amusement. It is rumored that Langston Hughes grew weary of Charlotte's downtown scene and moved back uptown to continue his love affair with Harlem. He eventually purchased a brownstone home at 20 West 127th Street, where he wrote freely and enjoyed the street life of Lenox Avenue.

Ordinary People

But the 1920s and 1930s were not especially good times for the ordinary, unskilled, working class of black Harlem. The average black person had a difficult time paying rent and putting food on the table. From 1917 until the early 1940s, most blacks in Harlem were barely holding on to family lifestyles rooted in Southern traditions. The influx of veterans from World War I in 1919, the economic instability caused by the Wall Street crash of 1927, the repeal of the Prohibition Act in 1933 (which dimmed Swing Street by 1940), and the great migration of black Southerners pushed the already fragile Harlem economic base beyond its healthy limit.

Unemployed Husbands with Employed Wives

Finding work in the industrialized cities required skills that most Southern black men and women did not have. Because of the huge number of uneducated Irish and Italian lower-class male immigrants, the basic unskilled jobs were taken and kept within their ranks. However, for the black female seeking domestic work and child care jobs, it was a different story. Domestic skills were the same in the North as they had been in the South. Transplanted Southern women found housing and work with children and the elderly more easily than equally unskilled black men. Day work was available, and the pay was cheap for women. However, it was never enough to sustain the extremely high rents charged for deplorable living conditions.

According to data within a report by Clyde V. Kiser, "Diminishing Family Income in Harlem: A Survey by Milbank Memorial Fund in 1933: A Possible Cause of the Harlem Riot," conditions in Harlem for 2,061 households living between 126th Street and 135th Street between Lenox and Seventh represented average or middling incomes surveyed.

> Even in 1929 the median family income of the unskilled laborers was approximately only $1,600 (a year). In 1932 the median income for families of this class fell to $907. This means that 50% of these families had incomes of less than $75 per month. In fact, slightly more than one quarter of them had incomes of less than $50 per month.

The disparity between blacks in the professional class—which included ministers, lawyers, doctors, teachers, professional musicians and artists, and white-collar proprietors—was tremendous.

In this group, the highest 1929 median
family income was $2,250 (a year) among
the proprietors. In 1932 the professional
class showed the highest median income
and this amounted to only $1,440 or
$120 per month.

An interesting twist for the black professional class
was its constituency. Approximately one-half were
musicians (jazz), one-fifth were ministers, and
undertakers accounted for one-eighth. All of the
black doctors, lawyers, teachers, and dentists were
within the small remaining percentage. Black jazz
musicians made more money between 1929 and
1933 than any other Harlem household.

Almost all professionals were men. Most of the black
professional men in Harlem lived a lifestyle foreign to the
unskilled working class. Unknowingly, many socially
unhealthy patterns of communication began to develop
between income and skill groups within Harlem's small
geographic location. The two separate black classes of
households, the "haves" and "have nots," which was
documented in the Milbank Report in the 1920s, set
the stage for the survival of black households.

Black women could live "on the place" as live-in
maids without too much trouble, and they would

visit their husbands or families on their day off. Thousands of black women sustained home life in this manner until the 1950s and paid rent for their aging mothers and grandmothers to care for their children. Having a place to call home was a basic for Harlem women, even if her husband had given up trying to get a job and accepted being the lowest man paid for the hardest job done. The Depression, beginning in 1927, forced all American men—black, white, and immigrant—to fight over the dwindling number of low-paying, unskilled jobs available.

It was the black woman's carry-all shopping bag that literally brought home the ham bone, chicken frame, and beef scraps to make a pot of her family's beans and greens flavorful with her skillet of cornbread.

All of the family wore hand-me-downs from discarded clothing from her boss. Her children were glad to wear ill-fitting shoes with good soles, and warm coats and sweaters to keep the unfamiliar Northern chill out of their Southern bones, regardless of the fit. Her man oftentimes wore the clothes from her employer's closet because it was the best he could do under the circumstances.

The black male's lack of employment opportunities made him unable to provide food, clothing, and shelter as he had done in the South. The urban economy created a generation of different Negro men, whose condition of underemployed or unemployed for the first time in their history in Africa or America rendered him vulnerable and devalued. Too many black men became dependent on their women, as were their children. His tenuous position slowly moved him out of his traditional position as head of the household, and he found her to have the muscle and power as the independent wage earner. The far-reaching implications of this dysfunctional equation proved to be a destructive force in their relationship.

Soon she forgot that the black American male's value as a worker during slavery was higher than that of cotton. Her man's body-per-dollar worth was the highest American gross national product. Maybe neither of them knew or forgot. Subsequently, her attention was forced to shift from being his woman to being the breadwinner.

The Swing Streets of Harlem during Prohibition did not make getting through the depressed years any easier. All over Harlem, alcohol was cheap—getting a drink was easier than finding employment. Watching self-absorbed, well-paid, suit-wearing jazzmen swagger up and out of places on their block during daylight hours when ordinary people went to work was probably not the best motivators to encourage black men to continue knocking on employers' doors that were closed to them. Holding on to manly pride must have been as hard on the block as it was with a black man's wife and children. The dynamics of the intimacy of their personal communication became askew when the balance of family power shifted, out of necessity for survival, from him to her as wage earner.

The New Negro male role became marginalized for the working-class Negro woman, while conceptually the black race was gaining ground politically. This was a critical, turnkey time for the black family, but there was nothing in place to put it back in balance. The concept of being a free individual in the North was bigger than the black man could deliver for his woman, children, or himself in the early 1900s. Unfortunately, freedom did not come with a guide book and training workshops; it just showed up.

For Harlem, the Prohibition Era was the best and worst of times, depending on one's situation. The black Harlem Renaissance scholars were writing poetry and books on slavery, and they were busy attacking the white man and segregation. The black jazz musicians were creating great music, and the dance floors were full of dancing feet. No one was paying attention to the mass destruction of the delicate, feminine qualities of the black female wife and mother—the soft sweetness of her spirit that was crucial for her man to experience if he was to continue to relate to her as his woman and not just a partner to pay bills. It was being corroded by society's denial of him to receive honest pay for an honest day's work. The Depression added a nail in the coffin that Prohibition had laid out for the Harlem household.

Masculinity and femininity, complimentary concepts in a loving relationship, were slaughtered after-hours on the Harlem city sidewalks. Black women were given the green light to do the heavy financial lifting as she skillfully performed the work at hand. Most white women, on the other hand, got to vote for politicians, evolved as individuals, had time for self-discovery and thereby tended to pursue adventures of the heart, spirit, and fantasy—as opposed to feeling responsible for feeding her man and children. Many became independent and were free to pursue happiness wherever it was found. Greenwich Village, Park Avenue, and Harlem became possibilities for fun.

The bruises left on the self-esteem of black women of the Prohibition and Depression eras are almost never discussed as being of psychological and social relevance to many current social and domestic issues. Back in the day, speakeasies were located within their blocks and housed in their buildings, and their leftover night crawlers pranced up and down their sidewalks, suffering from hangovers as they caught the bus to go to do a day's work. Jazz musicians and their followers lived out their newfound lifestyles under the watchful eyes of the black local women, who were likened to the backdrop scenery of *Porgy and Bess*, the Broadway musical. Except for the sex trade in the buffet flats or rent parties, little interaction took place that led to marriages; jazzmen had too many fish they could fry.

Negro showgirls had the double whammy. To be competitive in the chorus line, they were required to be young and "unofficially white without portfolio." Life for them on the stage was a tightrope. Their light skin, soft hair, and cash-paying occupations made them a threat to other black women. Churchgoing women in the tenements kept "the loose showgirls and club women" well away from their men if possible.

Showgirls were welcome as paying room renters with eating privileges, but the line was drawn between them and families. Many were from out of town, seeking to make a name for themselves as a lead singer or actress in a Broadway play. Their light and bright color was the primary barrier between trusting relationships with neighbors, peer groups, and even sometimes within families, where children were like rainbows.

One summer many years ago, I had an opportunity to meet a former Cotton Club dancer who shared a picture album with me. I listened to the stories of Lena Horne, Bill Robinson, Josephine Baker, and of her life as a Negro showgirl in the chorus line; it reinforced my compassion for the stressful situation caused by skin color between Negro women over men. Although her dancing career was near the end of the 1930s, her life as a "high yella" black showgirl was full of despair over the hatred displayed by other Negro women whenever she and her husband, who was a very dark black man, went out in basic black neighborhoods to eat or walk around in the park.

She told me of living with continuous stares of contempt and disgust openly flashed like daggers by black women—never black men. Her bright light skin and flashy clothes, jewelry, and accessories forced her to live in small, private Harlem social circles during the Renaissance, because showgirls never made enough money to save for a home in the suburbs. They received more gifts and vacation trips than real cash money from men, who were usually married. Life was not as easy for them as it appeared.

Little of the intellectual enlightenment of the Renaissance scholars made a dent in the pain caused by senseless discrimination. The idea of any effort to put our community back to the way it was originally, in the name of gentrification, does not seem to be on the drawing board. All of the past was not always better. The fear of being pushed out of the best locations in Harlem, now that the community was showing signs of tremendous success, was an overriding issue. It is a misconception by urban renewal corporations seeking to brand a marketing slogan, "Harlem's Second Renaissance," that the current Harlem mood of blacks living uptown is stuck in nostalgia.

Rolling back the hands of time in Harlem to the past could never be considered advantageous to all black people. Harlem Renaissance racism was openly hurled into the faces of all blacks, even by well-intentioned whites who considered themselves to be liberal, thinking intellectuals. Because of the superficial proximity of blacks and whites in the Harlem community back then, and by occupying common spaces on sidewalks, buses, speakeasy clubs, and some cabarets, listening to black men playing jazz, many may have thought there was a mutual meeting of the races on a human relationship level uptown.

Unfortunately, Prohibition movies and television series present an urban New York City illusion of "happy niggers" in Harlem that is only a movie script. How happy could the working, educated Harlem residents have been as they watched white people go and come and spend money anywhere they wanted in their neighborhood? How was the implied "Whites Only" sign explained to their children and to themselves, as free adults in the North? What were the New Negroes to feel when landlords charged excessive rents, forcing their households to double up and combine their money to pay for housing? How happy were black women, who had to accept the gradual increase of black professional men escorting white women on their arms, while black women for the most part remained faithful to them?

Swing Street Was Wide Open

Historically, Swing Street set the stage for white women and black men to cross paths easily in Harlem while ignoring black women. Following this path, as I see it, there was as a social progression for the white woman to the black man. They were accessible to each other; they had time, space, alcohol, and marijuana in plentiful supply.

Timing is everything.

After reviewing the social time line of that era, in my opinion the sequence of events that set the stage for interracial relationships to flourish in Harlem artistic urban settings is as follows.

1. In 1920 the white woman got the right to vote, just in time for Prohibition and the Jazz Era! She cut her hair, raised her skirts, smoked and drank alcohol in public, and began a new and empowered life. Driving an automobile gave her the opportunity to explore new communities.
2. In 1920 segregated social clubs spread like wildfire, but black male jazzmen were employed to play there regularly. Black jazz musicians also played at Swing Street Harlem speakeasies, which were open to all races and genders all night.
3. White women went to speakeasies up and down Swing Street freely, and they loved dancing to black music into the early hours where black men were playing.

4. In 1920 black women did not show up in speakeasies generally, because they were giving rent parties and selling fried fish and chicken to pay for their rent. Most went to bed on Saturday night so that they could be in church on Sunday. Black women's money was not spent for drinks in speakeasies on their block. Swing Street was where they lived with their families; it was home.

5. Black male musicians and celebrities and white women were available to each other in a close, intimate environment where no social rules governed, and all parties selfishly fulfilled their own desires.

Herein lies the darker side of Swing Street—along with the implied intimacy between white women and black men, the tolerance of drug use, and the ability to do almost anything under the blind eye of the police—developed an indelible, permanent dark stain on how Harlem is perceived as a community. The haze of negativity lingers as if there's bad breath from cheap bathtub gin.

The fact is that some of the most amazing, genius jazz musicians of all time were alive, assembled together because of segregation, and produced and challenged each other in small speakeasies all night and into the morning. Imagine the high level of excitement this aroused in white women, who had never been allowed to share the raw feelings with blacks in any medium. Speakeasies were tiny and everybody was elbow to elbow. It was a personal relationship between the performer and the audience; customers were involved and not just observers.

That was and is the difference still. It's the magic of fantasy. Whites showed up and supported the magic of the arts. White women were able to slip back and forth between their daytime reality downtown life and then their dark, exotic adventures uptown late at night. The intensity of the speakeasies' jazz music and the mutual human curiosity opened the door for racial barriers to lessen. Men and women explored drugs, alcohol, and intimate feelings in the clubs and beyond. These women could also afford to pay for their fun and folly with the black working musicians. Having personal contact with the white man's prized trophy was possibly an added unconscious incentive for the black musicians.

The more subtle, urban racism's distinct color lines seamlessly covered all facets of life within the members of urban black communities. Like an expected inheritance, some Harlem blacks unconsciously accepted and adhered to the Cotton Club and Smalls color distinction with impunity. Unfortunately, the bright-color and good-hair distinction still remains an unspoken inherent divide within all the Harlem communities across America.

But there are a few signs of forward movement in Harlem. Money, success and the outrageous open display of material wealth, are fast becoming as important as color and hair. Unfortunately, many of us still respond strongly to light skin color first, and hair texture and its length next, and concern for the quality of a person's character is an afterthought.

This is where our culture remains stuck on stupid in the past and present. For example, although we are living in the post-Renaissance era, as of this writing very few contemporary celebrity black males—who happen to be gangsters, rappers, movie stars, musicians, media personalities, athletes, doctors, lawyers, or politicians—elect to marry a chocolate-brown, full-bodied woman with natural hair. Being beautiful, highly educated, and from a great family with money still does not qualify her as a bride for the majority of accomplished black men.

The Harlem Renaissance reinforced and sustained the female color divide. Its scholars did not fully take on this problem with vigor. We do not need a second time around for a failed model, myth, and skin-color complexes. If gentrification is to resemble a Renaissance revival, hopefully the single black woman will begin to show up as a wife enjoying the protective wing of her man, and not be the strong image of a support mechanism for her entire family. Muscles look good on him too. Being Wonder Woman can get tiresome and self-defeating.

Moving Past Harlem's Past to a New Day

The New Harlem I'm currently experiencing has the potential to step over the barriers of stagnation, in favor of a newly written, fresh chapter. Today's Harlem entrepreneurs form and host business networks in which they share ideas and marketing techniques, take courses and earn degrees in business and finance, and are knowledgeable of computers and smart phones. Most of all, there is more mutual respect and networking given between racial and gender groups in the entrepreneurial arena.

What was perceived early on of a "white takeover or white take-back" of Harlem has not come to pass. Gradually it became clear that shared space was the real deal that developed. The new people on the block were forced to join the complex and highly stratified infrastructure within the black community; there were too many highly educated professionals to be exported to the outer boroughs.

The most unique quality that attracts all people to Harlem is still in place. Harlem has unapologetic blackness within its fibers. The village is still in place but is beginning to tilt. No matter how many different hues of people are walking on the sidewalks, it has a sense of blackness about it. The walk is paced, casual, and relaxed. Walking in Harlem is more than transporting yourself around; it's a time to see and be seen. Black folks in Harlem like living around each other. In reality, well-educated, money-making, successful people make up the community along with the other dynamics in the general population.

Harlem is unlike other urban centers like Washington, DC (where blacks living in Georgetown sold out or fled en masse to big houses in Maryland's suburbs), or St. Louis (where blacks dashed to University City and the counties beyond in an effort to get away from less empowered blacks and in an attempt to be "better than" or as good as a white lifestyle). Atlanta is another good example of blacks saying they live there, but in reality they live in a neighboring suburb. What is amazing in most of the aforementioned cities is that the real estate prices in the once black neighborhoods have now escalated so high that the black folks who fled can't afford to come back to live with the new white gentry occupants. This will not happen in Harlem because there is a middle class willing to fight to stay; newcomers are welcome to join in.

The ties that bind us as a community to our spiritual links of the core concepts of Harlem blackness fostered "the back in the day" of the Harlem Renaissance, motivated by black scholars. Unfortunately, integration and assimilation have contaminated that level of spiritual, original core blackness of the Harlem community, and therefore the intellectual think tank of the Harlem Renaissance is no longer possible.

The collective wisdom and talents of Paul Robson, W. E. B. Du Bois, Charles S. Johnson, Jessie Fauset, Frederick Douglass, Countee Cullen, Alain Locke, Zora Neal Hurston, E. Franklin Frazier, James Weldon Johnson, Langston Hughes, and Madam C. J. Walker is currently conceptually and in reality nonexistent. It was the substance of the overwhelming preponderance of genius talents in one small geographic location at the same time period, which prevails as the basis for the moral black authority for Harlem to be perceived as the epicenter of black culture. This concentration of sage-level community black consciousness has never been duplicated anywhere else at any time in America. That's why the original Harlem Renaissance remains like fertile soil enriched in intellectual and artistic blackness along the streets of Harlem. However, keep in mind that much of this nostalgia reads better than it played out in reality. Myths hold the respected traditions of a culture in place; therefore, the Harlem Renaissance was necessary mental sunshine for blacks to hold on to during trying days.

Constructive Resurrection

Consequently, young and middle-aged blacks and whites alike, desiring to be a part of our unique Harlem community on the rise, took out mortgages and bought houses and condos. Commercial spaces were leased by black, brown, and white entrepreneurs, side by side. However, change came very fast, and like magic, Harlem was transformed. The changes were dramatic but positive for a diverse, generally middle-class population.

My husband Bill and I watched our community evolve with gold rush energy. It became a real estate bonanza, a land of opportunity. Urban blight was now embraced as a rare find. Business speculators, investors, home buyers, and renters dashed about with cameras and electronic handheld devices like bees near a honey cone, looking for a deal. The ugly frog was now a handsome black prince.

Abandoned, private, majestic brownstones; huge, multiple-unit buildings neglected by deadbeat landlords; and vacant lots filled with debris suddenly became valuable. It was like the Northern influx of carpetbaggers during reconstruction in the South, coming to town with bags of new cash for a flat economy. Banks lending fresh mortgage money and investors seeking a new market put together the perfect picture of an economic boom.

Bill Clinton's, pseudo but highly publicized move to 125th Street added the seal of approval to New York politics—and added more fuel to the fire. The huge photo op gave many jazz musicians like Jimmy Heath and Bill Saxton a chance to perform on stage at the Adam Clayton Powell State Office Building. Although Clinton professes to play the sax and to be a jazz lover, he has yet to become an advocate or to build an honest bridge with Harlem jazz musicians. Harlem is still waiting for him to really move in. Nonetheless, his popularity helped push Harlem real estate prices and the home ownership acceptability index into the big leagues. The perception of Bill Clinton renting an office on 125th Street translated into real dollars for the Harlem business community. Having a United States president doing business in Central Harlem and eating at Sylvia's was a great new vision to grasp. However, even though everyday people did not get a piece of the real estate pie, they did benefit from the numerous job opportunities, upgrades, and accessible community amenities.

Health spas, gyms, and bowling lanes opened. PathMark, Fairway, Associated, and other large chain grocery stores opened locally, and farmer's markets from upstate New York brought well-priced, healthy foods to neighborhoods. Drugstore chains of every description opened, and Target, Home Depot, Staples, Marshall's, International House Of Pancakes, and Applebee's were now in walking distance or accessible by public transportation. Starbuck's and Sylvia's were neighbors. The visual and functional community upgrades helped eased the Harlem community into a new attitude of acceptance. Things are different, but still with a vibrant black majority living day to day and calling it home.

When the winds of change blew across central Harlem fast and furious, the new face of Harlem business and new homeowners was now that of international blacks, Europeans, Middle Easterners, Asians, and Islanders. On 116th Street from Lenox Avenue to

Eighth Avenue, the African merchants and dwellers have carved out their own cultural diaspora. French is the first language of many black children who now attend public school with Harlem children, with whom they learn to speak English. This is good cross-cultural exposure for both groups.

The whites' interests and lifestyles, which include buying overpriced dogs that wear designer clothing, was not an initial Harlem cultural trend. But in the last few years, well-dressed small dogs being walked or carried has filtered into black Harlem female lifestyles. Costly designer dogs being carried by black women in signature dog bags are now commonplace on most streets. Eating, drinking, meeting, and greeting in decorative sidewalk cafés along Lenox and Malcolm X Boulevard, Seventh Avenue and Adam Clayton Powell Boulevard, and Eight Avenue and Frederick Douglass Boulevard has become more like "white" downtown and less uptown urban. The wide Lenox Avenue is starting look like the old-fashioned stroll again.

The motives of the European, American white, African, Latina, and Asian potential owners and tenants were very basic. They wanted to remain in Manhattan with affordable housing, to have great public transportation, and to be near Central Park, restaurants, and shopping. Harlem is a location. For them, it's just a great destination for living and setting up a profitable business in the center of Manhattan. In addition, they brought their own lifestyle and culture with them, as all people have done everywhere in the world. It is especially the eclectic nature of major urban communities that cities such as Paris, London, and New York City have in common; they are urban centers filled with culturally diverse populations.

Time passes, and new ways of living become a part of the present, preparing people for the future. Gentrification, like Prohibition, will produce outcomes that will affect the daily lives of future generations. Whenever a small group of men or women come together to impose their perception of a cultural uplifting to a community in need of rejuvenation, somewhere in the change, crucial threads will be cut, and the quilt of cultural unity will slowly disappear and become beige or gray. The bright, slamming, irregular colors, smells, sounds, and lifestyles will flatten out to blend into inoffensive, financially induced norms. Change guarantees different, but not necessarily better. Change is uncertainty for those not in control. Gentrification is planned cultural change.

CHAPTER EIGHT

Gentrified Harlem Motif

The winds of change were sweeping across New York City with a wide brush, painting on an old canvas with new colors. Change was evident throughout New York, but especially in Manhattan. History has a way of repeating itself in different time frames, in different ways, and in different places based on the same theme. In this case, it was the 9/11 attack, which caused massive death tolls and structural devastation in the most symbolic American icon in the world, New York City. Change cut like a sharp razor across the renowned skyline, leaving an ugly scar. Our lives were immediately thrown into fear and chaos as Manhattan Island was locked down tight. All bridges and tunnels were closed. New Yorkers were isolated, waiting for the next shoe to drop. We were collectively unhinged.

The ripple effect caused radical shifts in our behavior in many ways. New Yorkers felt vulnerable and actually became more caring toward each other. They had to rethink the way they lived. Our hometown was forever changed: the deep and gaping hole, the smell, the smoke, the settling of the ashes along our windowsills, and the pictures taped in our elevators and bulletin boards of our neighbors about who had reported to work, and who was killed the same day.

That September morning forced the ravages of war down my throat. It was personalized, as all wars have been, but in the United States, usually it's to strangers on television in strange, hard-to-pronounce locations. As Americans, we usually think of war as being televised. Being attacked by planes on a sunny morning happens to those "other people," in a faraway land.

For me, I became keenly aware that we lived history daily, and it's only considered historical if something unusual happens. My worldview changed and I was changed. I gained increased respect for my use of time. Being alive and aware of changes around me at the beginning of the new millennium and post 911 has put Harlem on my agenda in a different way.

Moving forward and rebuilding became the motivating energy driving the city toward the future. Human and financial resources were spent to re-establish stability and a comfort zone. The need for relocation for many people was obvious.

Gentrification Arrives with a Full Bag

New circumstances and plans ushered into Harlem, the center of Manhattan, a building boom of astronomical proportions. Very quickly, high-end apartment complexes and a huge wave of people renting and buying buildings erupted, and it was unprecedented. After the attack, which destroyed both World Trade Center buildings and surrounding buildings, the immediate neighborhood was left uninhabitable. The lower tip of Manhattan and the Battery Park area along the Hudson River became geographically undesirable.

The aftermath of 911 took a severe toll on a vibrant community at the southern tip of the city. Relocation was needed for some, mostly white New Yorkers and newcomers. Searching eyes looked northward to virgin Manhattan territory. Uptown in Harlem, located in Manhattan's center, and the most northern tip of Manhattan, Washington Heights, became the new hotspot neighborhoods. Tall cranes and cement trucks took over and filled the once open skyline with towering walls of glass, steel, and bricks. Caverns filled with dark shadows were created between blocks that once boasted open space. Sky, air, and light became scarce. Harlem sidewalks and street corners became battle zones, where space was at a premium.

Harlemites were compelled to accommodate the new and intense construction sites, and they learned to adapt to the building boom. The norm became senior citizens zipping around in motorized wheel chairs or hobbling on canes and walkers and parents pushing baby carriages, trying to make it to medical appointments at clinics around the detour signs of construction workers. School children and teens, in neat uniforms with overloaded back packs, mixed in with thousands of everyday New Yorkers, who were also trying to have a routine work day in the midst of rebuilding. The normal, day-to-day, Harlem lifestyle kept changing and pressing on as the landscape grew multilingual.

Gentrification or Whitewashing?

Most of us blacks feared that we would become ghosts of the past in the new plan consuming our neighborhood. Many of the physical excavations were happening on one side of the street, while multiplexes were rising on the other. Like an avalanche, it was all occurring rapidly in all directions. Although we were prepared for some community changes, we were blown away at the sheer volume of the new construction. Almost as astounding as the large number of new white residents was the overflowing number of Africans, newly arrived from the continent, who settled in on West 116th Street.

A decade of heated City Hall protest marches and neighborhood meetings at Planning Board Ten on 125th Street at least prepared us for the outrageously greedy takeover of our powerful Harlem neighbor, Columbia University. Columbia's expansion of their Harlem 106th Street campus area—and the additional property of the West Side from Broadway over to the Hudson River from 110th Street up to approximately 135th Street—was massive. The bottom line to any gentrification initiative is an attempt to introduce "a more gentile, higher culture" to an established community considered to be in need of uplifting. Harlem for sure needed an overhaul, but it did not need replacing.

On July 24, 2011, the Real News Network carried a typed transcript taken from a recording entitled "Columbia U., Race, Class and the Gentrification of Harlem." Its commentary is a public record between Nellie Hester Bailey, cofounder of Harlem Tenants Council, and David Dougherty of TRNNetwork. The following five recorded consecutive statements are located near the end of the transcript and reflect the overall sentiments expressed during the entire interview.

Bailey: Columbia University had its sights on all these private properties. But in order to jumpstart eminent domain, there has to be a finding of blight. So what did the university do? They allowed their property to become blighted so that the determination of blight would be found to jumpstart the eminent domain process. The public review process that is required for this confiscation was completely controlled by the university. And so it was a foregone conclusion what the results were going to be.

Dougherty: An active and enduring resistance has been born in Harlem in opposition to the expansion project and other motors of gentrification, as community members engage in protests and other forms of organizing. Some organizers like Nellie are concerned about the means by which institutions like Columbia University are able to use their influence and tax exempt status to manipulate levers of power through their connections with financial elites, real estate developers, and the state.

Bailey: President Bollinger, the President of Columbia University, also serves as the chair of the New York Federal Reserve. The Federal Reserve is one of the most powerful financial institutions in the country. One can easily surmise that they are in fact the shapers, the architects of the future of New York, both financially and residentially and commercially. They will determine, through the control in its relationship with the financial markets, what goes on here in New York City.

Dougherty: In addition to Columbia University's president's recently appointed role as chair to the New York Fed, there are also a number of other heavy movers in the school's current 24 member board of trustees. Among them are a number of high-level executives and some of the most powerful investment banks, including Goldman Sachs, Citigroup, And Bank of America Merrill Lynch. Also in the ranks of the board of trustees is the owner of a luxury New York City highrise real estate company, as well as a standing judge on the United States Court of Appeals' Second Circuit court.

Bailey: Columbia University is the key partner in deciding the future of New York City. They're not just an educational institution; they are one of the leaders of the city in deciding the course of growth and the development of this city and who stays and who doesn't. Real News Network transcript, "Columbia U., Race, Class and Gentrification of Harlem" carried July 24, 2011. Interview of Nellie Bailey, Co founder of Harlem Tenants Council.

After reading the complete interview thoroughly several times, I was left with a phrase used by Nellie Bailey: "What's happening in Harlem is happening in the Bronx and Bedford-Stuyvesant, where these communities are being lost, where people are being driven out by public policy, which is really about ethnic cleansing." The introduction of the concept of ethnic cleansing placed a very cold and dangerous face on gentrification, where black culture could possibly suffer from blight and eventually become white by default.

Raising the issue of racial cleansing in the Harlem community pushes buttons that need to be addressed but not become a focal point. Otherwise, the sustaining strength of Africans' heritage that survived almost a half century of slavery can be snuffed out like victims of a plague. Replacing abandoned buildings with luxury towers and providing state-of-the-art shops and restaurants within a community are the obvious attributes to accompany gentrification. It's what the eye can readily see.

Racial cleansing can only take place if the people give up on themselves and choose to become victims of the well-financed, invasive culture. White people can move in, but black culture is Harlem. Harlem's community culture is deeper than buildings and real estate. Its culture has a seamless transparency that is often confused with convenient, eager news bites describing drugs, crime, and poverty in Harlem. Ethnicity is culture. Culture is the reality of what the people do from day to day. Blacks actually live uptown and will not be cleansed or bleached out by developers.

Old men gathering around talking, still girl watching and listening to old tales; drummers playing codes of communication; chess players competing across boards on stone tables in the parks; shirtless black and tan boys sweating through a pickup basketball game, with young girls watching them while the music beats the air; women in stylish shoes carrying overly large handbags and wearing the latest hairstyles and clothing on their way to work while chatting on the cell phone—all this is commonplace. The man standing next to her on the busy corner, impeccably dressed for success while sending a text, politely allows her to slip past him to go down the subway stairs as soon as the light flashes to walk. Now he can watch her walk from behind and decide on his next move, just in case he sees her again at the Red Rooster after work, or the Studio Museum on Sunday afternoon.

Black people in Harlem have a mutual ethnic life rhythm that will not be lost in gentrification's translations. Nellie Bailey can relax but remain a diligent gatekeeper and community stakeholder. Black culture in Harlem, in my opinion, is changing with progress but is not disappearing. Harlem has simply changed.

Leon James Bynum, a young writer from the Columbia University establishment, published with the National Dialogue on "Race Relations Lecture Notes and Thoughtful Questions Subheading: Community."

Title: Harlem's Continuing Gentrification and Intraracial Relations

During the 1990's, the number of middle and upper-middle class households in Harlem increased by thirty-five percent. The number of professionals, individuals with higher education, and homeowners all increased in those communities. Community boards in Harlem advocated developments out of the price range of longtime Harlemites, indicating that they supported driving up Harlem's housing market, thereby displacing them. The concerns of the African-American middle class in both neighborhoods typically have not included maintaining a comfortable way of life for the poorest members of the community. As a result, intra racial animus can be observed emanating from both sides.

Some longtime residents see the middle class blacks who promote development as bringing positive new opportunities to the community. Others label them as sell-outs. Because the African-American middle class is less secure than their white counterparts, they have to work much harder and act more stringently to protect their investment and social

status, Class differences keep political
unity fractured.

In spite of differences, as mentioned above by Bynum, between the blacks in lower, middle, and upper-middle classes and their interests in the community, the common denominator of race is a stronger bond than the economic differences. The proximity of the NYC housing projects and the subsidized housing keeps the black condo and brownstone owners close. Touching elbows and walking to the same beat on the same sidewalks goes a long way to keep a culture intact.

A little in-house friction keeps it active and fresh. The concerns of Lee Bynum are too often swept under the table. Yes, highly educated black people with money live in Harlem. Yes, undereducated black people without economic stability live in Harlem. The media image dwells 99 percent on the latter. But we need to be reminded that there are valid differences within the black race that are powerful enough to separate us, if we permit our communication to become shallow and dismissive.

We are blessed to live "up close and personal" in Harlem. Gentrification can and will serve our community, as long as we keep control of what they want. Columbia University and corporations will never have our black creativity, and that's what 100 percent of the tourists come to Harlem to experience. They're still curiously fascinated by our ability to set style trends in all aspects of fashion, music, dance, art, and language; we set the standard for cool. Harlem's black culture is resistant to cleansing.

Now seems to be the time for the long-suffering black Harlem stakeholders and landlords to get a shot at enjoying the benefit of their tax dollars and increased land value on their real estate holdings. The impressive number of black Harlem homeowners who persevered during the darkest era was pleasantly surprised at the new Harlem that materialized like a midwestern tornado.

The economic tide turned advantageously toward the solid middle- and upper-class Harlemites who would have access to the quality of life they expected to enjoy in their own neighborhood, where they are heavily invested. Spending money uptown in the local community is now a first choice.

The blatant shift in focus of 125th Street and of 116th Street has been breathtaking. At the most eastern tip of both streets approaching the Harlem River Drive now stands a giant shopping mall with indoor parking. Each new site not only generated a beneficial facelift for underutilized property, but more important it created full-time, permanent jobs, with benefits for many Harlem and Bronx employees.

In the opposite direction, going west on 125th Street to the banks of the Hudson River is perhaps the most impressive change. The development of the Harlem pier and boat basin is not only a beautiful, green, people-friendly, open space, for bench sitting, leisure conservations, boat watching, reading, or fishing from the pier; it is the perfect bikers' rest stop. Great restaurants and outdoor cafés are highly accessible by bike, car, or 125th Street and Broadway subway trains. Mayor Bloomberg's preoccupation with biking has created paved bike paths almost fully around the perimeter of Manhattan Island. Bikers traveling the paved path between the George Washington Bridge (north end) and Battery Park (south end) are now able to spend time, have lunch, and hang out in the newly developed 125th Street Harlem waterfront.

The wonderfully, revived version of the old Cotton Club from 132nd Street is still around. The new location near West 125th Street and near Claremont Avenue the Hudson River Pier area has changed, but the flavor is Harlem-style charm. Its owner, John, is a smart black businessman who owns his business and runs a smooth, tight ship. Gentrification has not closed him down, and white customers are welcome to come in and sit next to blacks and swing dance to big band music like back in the day.

Harlem looks and feels like good times may be just around the next corner of the new condos on the Gold Coast in Soha (South Harlem, if you don't mind), or at Bill's Place on Swing Street. Change is good for Harlem, and all Harlemites can enjoy the new benefits while missing the old. Fear is a natural by-product of change. Moving forward into the unknown is not comfortable for individuals, communities, or organizations; all of the players try to protect their investments and assets to guarantee longevity in the newly developed scenario.

Gentrification is an experiment that has large consequences on all sides. Harlem's black people survived the Great Depression, Prohibition, and the heroine massacre, and now gentrification is here. I'm optimistic about Harlem's future. The Harlem street scenes are changing faster than can be discussed over a hot cup of Starbuck's or Dunkin' Donuts coffee or green tea.

116th and 7th Avenue /
Frederick Douglass Boulevard

118th Street and St. Nicholas Avenue

125th Street and Lenox Avenue (Malcolm X
Boulevard), NW corner

125th Street and Lenox Avenue (Malcolm X
Boulevard), NE corner

Lenox Avenue (Malcolm X Boulevard), between
126th and 127th Streets

Lenox Avenue (Malcolm X Boulevard), between
126th and 127th Streets

Magic Johnson Theatres, 8th Avenue (Frederick
Douglass Boulevard), and 124th Street, NW corner

125th Street, 8th Avenue (Frederick Douglass
Boulevard), and 124th Street, NW corner

Smalls Paradise Lounge, 135th and 7th Avenue
(Adam Clayton Powell Boulevard), SW corner

8th Avenue, between 137th and 138th Streets

145th Street and Bradhurst Avenue, SE corner

145th Street and Bradhurst Avenue,
NE corner

110th Street, Duke Ellington Circle at
5th Avenue, Central Park

John Hick's Way, West 139th Street
and 8th Avenue

CHAPTER NINE

The Harlem Jazz Scene

Jazz has managed to survive in spite of the shortcomings of the Renaissance and the wrecking ball of gentrification. It's tight and tough. Jazz is like a black church sermon: it has staying power, and it's at its best when it gets a live response. Like a black preacher, the more informed the members are of the scriptures, the more soulfully they respond to the call of the preacher. Sermons have almost supernatural effects of euphoria on the membership. Ministers frequently sweat and prance around. The Holy Ghost has been known to appear and make members jump around and shout out loud. The church sometimes seems to rock.

Jazz is almost identical. The more knowledgeable the listeners are in the audience, the more responsive they are to certain familiar musical improvisational skills. Call and response creates the mood that is free of constraints of the written notes. Great musicians' improvisations create a journey and a surprise adventure that ends in a hot, sweaty place where soul and cool live in tandem. Jazz ecstasy has been known to make audiences smile, shake their heads, and get on their feet to dance. However, jazz musicians always remain cool; even when they swing, they stay cool.

Live entertainment venues lingered far behind the restaurant and other commercial and retail business establishments. Few if any dance clubs opened with spacious floors for dancing. Live entertainment was confined to only a few locations, and few of them accommodated dancing at all. The entertainment scene was scarce, and venues to hear jazz had dried up significantly throughout the city, especially in Harlem. Talented jazz musicians who liked performing uptown were forced to scramble and play musical chairs between a few venues catering to jazz. The domino effect became a common occurrence throughout the jazz scene. Black club and restaurant owners who had traditionally supported live jazz began to fold up without community protests or visible signs of indignation.

Jazz Joints Are Closing

It was as if the veteran owners were oblivious of the change of the color guard uptown, and they continued to operate under the old-school mentality of just running a spot. Maybe some of them were so caught up in the large increase in traffic and tour groups filling their places that they failed to pay attention to the increase in the cost to do business uptown—especially if purchasing the real estate housing one's business was not a priority, because it was dirt cheap. Instead of buying, many of them signed long-term leases with good rates. This made the profit margin good for years, but gentrification showed its veracious appetite for prime real estate. For many, to re-sign a new lease became extremely costly and out of reach.

Some businesses closed their doors because of the stress of keeping up with the new way of doing business. Harlem's market and customer base was new and demanding. No one had the corner on the market, and competition was alive and well. Unfortunately, jazz has suffered the loss of a few standards and new kids on the block.

St. Nick's Pub

St. Nick's Pub at West 149th Street and St. Nicholas Avenue has been closed since 2010 as a full-time jazz joint. It was a seedy, dark, lower-level, narrow place that looked like a scene from a New York urban film. It had the street characters hanging out on the corners and less than inviting signs and entrance.

The long bar on the right wall dominated, and tables and chairs of some combination filled in the area in front of the stage.

An array of things and colored strings of lights swung from the ceiling across a huge, larger-than-life wall hanging of Miles Davis. It did not hang securely or straight, but Miles's presence on the worn poster served as an excellent backdrop for a seedy jazz joint. What the place lacked in décor, it more than made up for with interesting characters.

A musical tradition was the jazz provided by the Sugar Hill Band with Patience Higgins, Marcus Perciani, Eli Fantain, Dave Gibson, and the late Andy McCloud, who played for many years to full houses and appreciative audiences. They were blessed to have Berta as a faithful jazz supporter.

For ten years Bill Saxton developed his style of jazz presence, which drew musicians nationally and internationally to his sessions. Bill's Fridays night shows guaranteed a packed house and guest jazz celebrities. I gave him a birthday party once with an exotic dancer, Karla Jones, and people were standing on top of cars outside in the street trying to see inside. It was that kind of a joint. Frank and Cecelia Foster and Bobby and Pam Watson were guests. Dion Parsons and Bobby Forrester were in Bill Saxton's Trio. The pub had the dark edge that lent itself to great live jazz. A wonderful woman, Celeste Sapp, was the manager. Because of her style and personality, the pub was able to maintain itself as a stable Harlem jazz venue for many years.

Earl Spain closed out his lease and shut the doors to the jazz at the pub, and he went farther downtown to a premier jazz venue, which had been closed for over fifteen years. He and Celeste reopened Minton's Playhouse for a very brief and uneventful run.

Minton's Playhouse

Minton's was at West 118th Street, between St. Nicholas and Seventh Avenues. After being closed for over thirty years, it reopened and then closed within two years, in 2010. Minton's has no comparable rival exclusive jazz venue that touches its historic place for black jazz musicians. Not only is it large in size and has a lower level, but it is full of stories of the lives of the men and women who gave up so much music within the walls. Thelonious Monk, Bud Powell, Max Roach, Kenny Clark, Roy Haynes, Charles Mingus, Tommy Potter, Charles Parker, Dizzy Gillespie, John Coltrane, Miles Davis, Kenny Durham, and Billie Holliday—the list goes on and on. This coveted group of musicians was together at the same place and at a high level of musicianship for over twenty-five years. The mural on the wall of the stage is a much-photographed classic. The young Bill Saxton was given a chance to play at a jam session hosted by Kenny Durham in the late 1970s.

The Lenox Lounge

As of this writing, the Lenox Lounge, located on Lenox Avenue between 125th and 124th Streets, has been cited in news articles about the closing of its doors on December 31, 2012. The Sugar Hill Band and other house musicians and bar staff have been given final notice. The Lenox Lounge is the only remaining key venue left with connection to all the nostalgia as well as current jazz activity. Time will tell the story of Al "Buster" Reed, the black lessee, as he plays out his Harlem history. Mr. Reed closed the Lenox Lounge doors on New Year's Eve, 2012. Subsequently he had the historic neon signs and exterior removed. Chains and padlocks are now on the closed doors. Again, Harlem ghosts of a by-gone era were left behind.

The young black owners are said to be negotiating with many other interested parties, and Mr. Reed is leasing a space a couple blocks up on Lenox Avenue and will open another business in the midst of lawsuits and court appearances. To Reed's credit, some years ago he hired Ms. Sharron Cannon to manage and increase his audience capacity and live jazz music program.

Not only did Ms. Cannon heighten the quality of the lounge's live entertainment line up, but she took care of a crucial business detail. Before she left her managerial position, she applied for and secured the trademark for herself, Sharron Cannon, and Mr. Al Reed. Now he is safe from outsiders taking Lenox Lounge usage away from his control.

No, a white millionaire did not put Lenox Lounge out of business. A young, hard-working black couple of modest means was smart enough to buy the old, short, two-storied building that housed the Lenox Lounge, back in the day when everything was for sale in Harlem for a song and a dance.

No, it wasn't an Asian or European invader takeover rumor, likened to the ignorant, gossiping sources who love to hate about Sylvia's. The Woods family was smart enough years ago to buy their buildings and become the landlord themselves. Sylvia's new, young generation is still in business with busloads of tourists at their open doors. Black folks love to gossip uptown about things they "heard" but know nothing about.

St. Nick's Pub, 149th and St. Nicholas Avenue,
SW corner

Minton's Playhouse, 118th Street, between 7th
Avenue and St. Nicholas Avenue

Minton's Playhouse, 118th Street, between 7th Avenue and St. Nicholas Avenue

Lenox Lounge open, Lenox Avenue (Malcolm X
Boulevard), between 125th Street

Lenox Lounge closed, Lenox Avenue (Malcolm X
Boulevard), between 125th and 124th Streets

Renaissance Ballroom closed, 138th Street,
between 7th Lenox Avenues

CHAPTER TEN

Along Comes Bill

Harlem Bound

I had learned to love Harlem as a child, from my father, Theodore. He regularly read to us from his once white leather scrapbook. Before I fully understood politics and entertainers, and I heard about news of Harlem from newspaper articles. He told us stories of the larger-than-life giants Reverend Adam Clayton Powell Jr., Paul Robson, Mary Bethune, Ralph Bunche, and A. Phillip Randolph, who were the political champions, and of Duke Ellington, Count Basie, Billie Holiday, and Ella Fitzgerald, his musical favorites.

And then there was Joe Louis fighting in Madison Square Garden; it happened on the radio in our living room too. There were pictures of a bar named the Brown Bomber, on St. Nicholas Avenue at 145th Street, and it was the best ever. Harlem culture lived through my daddy, who was a race man and loved political issues pertaining to the Negro, jazz, and all the drama that went with them.

Back then, we had a beautiful Philco combination radio and automatic changing record player. After dinner, Daddy played the most exciting music and we danced. He loved to dance on the big floors of ballrooms and dance halls, and I was his at-home partner. He was big on smooth, offbeat moves and graceful turns. He put on big 78 records, which were kept in paper jackets with a hole in the middle to show the colorful title peeping through. The pages of manila record jackets were kept in sturdily bound, hardcover albums; these albums were handled as if they were sacred books. The album cover pictures of glamorous singers and musicians kept me mesmerized as the scratchy sounds from the thick needle wound its way through the deep, coarse grooves, releasing magic sounds.

Best of all were the full stories and biographies enclosed. Theodore used them as teaching opportunities with my brother, Joseph; sister, Paulette; and me. But nothing came close to his firsthand accounts from Club Riviera on Delmar; it was the Apollo of Harlem. I still have an original autograph from Ella Fitzgerald scribbled on the back of his club photograph cover.

Every now and then there would be a live broadcast, and we could hear the whole show. Radio was great training for my imagination. Duke, Basie, and our locals Jimmy Forest and Oliver Nelson were great records to train my young ears, and my feet to enjoy dance rhythms. Daddy put on Billie, Ella, Nat King Cole, and other singers who painted stories. I could close my eyes to see color and feel mood while learning to listen in the living room of our second-floor flat, which was downtown in the better part of the hood, on Thomas Street near Leffingwell.

My mother, Pauline, and sister, Paulette, preferred the blues; they loved Little Willie John. My brother, Joe, played the bass in the Vashon High School jazz band. But, in my head, I imagined I was "Stompin' at the Savoy" with a handsome young New York dance partner, with my wide skirt flying high. Our house encouraged pragmatic dreamers; a love for music, history, and dance was my staple.

Dad was an early NAACP community organizer, and his father, Alzo Palmer, was a Pullman porter and a supporter of America's first official Negro trade union protest of the Sleeping Car Porters Union against the railroad. The spirit of high self-esteem and standards were stamped into my young, impressionable brain by role models whom I lived with daily. Theodore gave me graceful moves on the dance floor and guts for the street, along with a good name that I happen to like.

I arrived in Harlem in 1962. The recently built Lenox Terrace at 2186 Fifth Avenue had a uniformed doorman. He helped me with my bags and announced my arrival to my big brother and his drop-dead gorgeous wife, Elaine. I felt like I had died and gone to heaven. Harlem was now my new home, and I was unknowingly fully prepared to be an active resident. I had been carefully raised and bound in layers of God's armor from a long line of Mississippi slave ancestors. What was I to fear?

Now I could see Theodore's scrapbook for myself. Little did I know that the plethora of clubs that lined the avenues were on their way out. I had missed Harlem's heyday. Red Rooster, Jaques, Count Basie's, the Baby Grand, Club Barron, Smalls Paradise, Savoy Ballroom, Selbra's Midway Lounge, the Renny, Salt and Pepper, Gold Brick, Bell Book and Candle, Carl's Corner, Allen's Alley, Paradise, Mark Four, Blue Book, Diggs Den, the Brown Bomber, and the Big Apple were beginning to dim their lights. I missed the Roaring

Twenties completely and caught the tail end of the sixties main drag. I felt cheated. I didn't get a chance to turn myself upside down and inside out, dancing on the great ballroom fast track wooden floor. My visions of flipping and swinging over and around the shoulders of a tall, dark, and handsome New York smooth hoofer were denied. I could have done it.

Timing is everything.

But all was not lost; I was just in time for the disco-era downtown clubs. I wholeheartedly bought into the trendy uniform: skin-tight hot pants and jumpsuits, thigh-high platform boots, nappy afro, and big earrings. To my brother's dismay, I was mesmerized by the turning glass ball and the booming DJ while dancing the nights away with Donna Summer and Parliament Funkadelic. I became electronically wired for sound, especially if it was loud.

I stayed dancing in club orbits for years. I had missed the big band swing dance halls, but I got every inch of sweat and booty shaking possible out of the Studio 54, Xenon's, Cheetah, and Electric Circus downtown to Casablanca, on the Upper West Side. It was loud and brash and lacked elegance, but it was great fun and full of aerobic benefits that left my hearing diminished. Listening to the music for quality musicianship was not the objective; it was about the moves to the groove.

Like clockwork, my professional life as an educator and arts administrator began promptly and ran from 8:30 a.m. until 5:00 p.m. daily. My social schedule and most of my professional friends adopted timetables based on their daytime work.

The closing and decline of dance clubs changed the weekend party habits of my aging generation of New York nightlife. Some resorted to house parties, and many began to frequent bars and lounges. Although the DJs kept the dying disco era alive as long as possible, the music was never substantial enough to become stabilized with a regular fan base to support itself in Harlem.

Presently, dancing uptown in Harlem operates on the fringe of other venues. There is not one dance hall dedicated to swing or freestyle or popular dancing, as it was during the Jazz Era. Hopefully, gentrification will bring dancing feet back to Harlem. However, jazz music has always remained a steady and consistent staple in New York, and especially Harlem. Gentrification has changed the face of how it is presented by opening a few high-end restaurants that offer live music in general, while not specifying jazz as the main genre of entertainment. Subsequently, jazz venues are on the decline uptown.

The subtle but slow decline of jazz music venues in Harlem did not really get my attention until I quite casually met Bill Saxton. On my way to a party, I briefly stopped by to wish a friend happy birthday at Showman's on West 125th Street. After a quick greeting to Joe and the barmaid, my friend Barbara Thomas and I were leaving when a polite, well-dressed man introduced himself to me as Bill Saxton. I thought he was just another party guest being friendly. After a pleasant conversation and a few New York style parting kisses, we left as quickly as we came.

Months later, Barbara and I saw him again at the same place; coincidentally, we knew some of the same people who were regulars there having drinks at the bar. We stayed there longer than planned, and I was reintroduced to Bill Saxton and was told he was an excellent jazz musician by my friend Lilian Pierce, the barmaid and major personality at Showman's. I did not know him.

Taking into account how I had spent over twenty five years of my professional career and social nightlife and the manner in which Bill spent all of his work life, there was no way for our paths to have crossed.

I did not know that he was a musician. Neither did I know he lived only a block and a half from my apartment on Central Park West. We were neighbors. I worked in creative arts quietly during the day, and he worked nights making music with jazz bands, playing the sax.

We had fun getting to know each other. I thought his life, in and out of cities and countries, was insane, and he thought my stability in NYC was boring. Our conversations were planets apart but within the same artistic galaxy. He was convinced he was smarter than most, and I thought I was certainly brighter than sunshine. We were like oil and water for the most part. We were secure in our chosen fields of work, had always earned a living as creative individuals, and loved being independent.

Our biggest mutual attraction was our fearless attitudes toward conquering whatever life could put in our way. Although we were from very different cuts of cloth, we were woven the same basic fibers. Our oil and water meshed into a complex but smooth balm. Bill's positive attitude toward being a hands-on single father and the fact that he shopped with coupons on sale days nailed my attention. Was this smart, cooler than cool black man in dark glasses, alligator shoes, and stingy brim hat for real?

We became good friends and started to seriously date. Our love life grew into a mission statement. It was a mandate. There was always something major to do.

Meeting Bill Saxton was the equivalent to taking a college course in jazz appreciation that somehow always ended up in Harlem. His social itinerary was very limited for my social party mentality and taste. All of our dates were jazz related—either listening to someone play jazz or listening to him play jazz with others before or after a great dinner became standard procedure. It was jazz, jazz, and more jazz. This was out of my comfort zone, but love conquers all. Slowly the music returned me to a familiar place, where I was happy as a child, to the secure place where I learned to dance to big band records. Now, occasionally I can enjoy swing dance to the live big bands of the Harlem Renaissance and the wonderful Charles Tolliver Big Band. For a great fun night out, we enjoy live big bands at lavish parties given by George Aprile at his Bogardus Mansion downtown. To my surprise, Bill turned out to be a good dance partner, especially on Latin tunes. God is good.

About Bill

Bill has never really left the Harlem Hospital area, where he was born on June 28, 1946. The place he called home, for most of his young years was 2534 Seventh Avenue. His life experiences in apartment 12, on the top-floor walk-up, serves as his frame of reference, where he formulated his worldview. Watching his young mother's determination to raise her family as a unit, with pride and dignity, burned deep wounds in his innocent childhood. Although deserted by her husband, Norman Saxton, the young, pretty Clarise became resourceful and tenacious. She decided that their children Marie, Pete, Billie, Michael and Wendy, would get the best of what was available, from a bad situation. Clarise's daily struggles to create interesting dishes from basic food, and her ability to magnificently iron to silky smooth their most basic clothing, and her pain when she could stretch her dollars no further, was almost unbearable. The young mother performed miracles. Christmas Day and Easter Sundays, wore into their household budget like salt in an open wound. But no matter what, they all had strong family loving support to feel good about themselves. Their close family made a good life for themselves during harsh times. The Saxton children were closely knit into a strong unit.

As a very young teenager, Bill was denied fundamental entitlements afforded to most children in school, because of domestic circumstances that caused severe financial hardships. Early on he had the ability to humble himself when faced with the unacceptable, so that the final results would become acceptable without shame. When handed a lemon, he reserved the choice to make lemonade or sell to the lemon. He personalized his poverty so deeply that his level of human veracity is only exceeded by his musical talent.

One case in point was in 1963. It was class picture day at Frederick Douglass Jr. High School, at 139th Street near Lenox Avenue. He did not have an appropriate shirt with a collar for the yearbook photograph, but he was determined to be photographed with his class. His friend and classmate, Lenny Carpenter, who lived in the Harlem River Houses, loaned Bill his shirt to wear after he had finished taking his picture in it. Both Lenny and Bill were in the same shirt on the same page in the Douglass Year Book. Bill has a Kool-Aid smile on his face and a gleam in his eye. He did it.

But home was a love affair. Clarise Saxton had a joyful house. The living room found neighbors and relatives listening to music, laughing, and talking. Billie was always the entrepreneur of the family. When Bill was eighteen months old, his mother's friends were amused by his uncanny ability to hear a song and later go through a pile of records and pick out the correct song. At his young age, he paid close attention to what he heard and saw. Billie could distinguish what he heard and associated it the artist that was on a particular record label. Someone would challenge him to find their request, and they gave him a tip or treat. When he was older, Billie sang their favorites and received larger tips. He had a hustle in his living room as soon as he could walk. He liked the excitement of performing and getting attention, and most of all getting paid. However, nothing beat the excitement of Clarise hitting the number, single action, boxed, or straight; it was a fun time for a few days. It was better than all the holidays put together. It was cash money in the house.

With so many families having children about the same age in the neighborhood, there were clusters of youngsters of all age groups for fun and protection. Bill, Larry, and Cody and this large crew banded together to explore every back yard in the block, hillsides, and trails in Colonial Park (Jackie Robinson). They sneaked in the pool during hot summer days, made scooters from skates nailed to old boards, and rode nonstop down the 142 Street hill from Amsterdam to Edgecombe Avenue. When they were at the top of the 142th Street hill, it never occurred to them to walk across the street and explore the lovely campus grounds of New York City College; neither did they think that they could be killed in traffic.

His young crew felt ownership to whatever they could think of to get into. One of their regular routes was the huge, 146th Street and Lenox Avenue NYC transit bus garage and terminal, where drivers reported for duty. During a shift change, a driver left the engine running in one of the parked buses. Bill and his teen crew boarded the bus—Bill took the driver's seat—and drove the bus down Lenox Avenue. After several blocks, he and his friends jumped off, ran like hell, and left the bus idling at a curb. He was fifteen at the time.

The Harlem Fire

Bill's resourceful mother had to relocate the family to the Burauch Houses, near Huston Street and down to the Lower East Side, because of a severe fire in their tenement building caused by a habitually careless neighbor. Moving from Seventh Avenue was a double-edged sword. Although Clarise had a lovely apartment in a very well-maintained building, and they would not miss the long walk up five flights or the tepid radiators in winter, she and her family would miss a huge piece of the history they called home. It was taken away forever; fire destroys everything but memories.

Gone were the stoop stories by brother Pete, telling of witnessing John Coltrane playing "My Favorite Things" at the Apollo nonstop for over an hour. Gone were his adolescent crew having discussions of flying pigeons from the roof, summer days of making a bike out of spare parts, lies told of making out with girls, schoolyard basketball games, hustling grocery deliveries to make movie money or to buy three rock cakes for a quarter at the West Indian bakery on Eighth Avenue near 146th Street. His building's stoop was the official seat of gossip and communication; it was the control center. Gone was being called Billie; he became Bill.

His Harlem stoop had a defined function: it was the first line of defense for all who lived in the building. At an early age, he learned in Harlem that no matter what was going down, if you made it to the stoop of your building, you were home free with nothing to worry about. Bill had grown up feeling secure and powerful on his home block. Boys became men there.

Uptown, everything was just a few steps away from his stoop. Bill enjoyed walking on the Seventh Avenue strip, past joints like Jacques, the Red Rooster, Smalls Paradise, and Count Basie's, where great jazz music spilled out onto sidewalks lined with hustlers wearing huge jewelry and hats, as ostentatious as their long cars that were perfectly double parked. It was a reviewing stand and daily ritual for the "street niggas" with long money to come together to confirm their status and relationships. It was still the African village square, as it happens instinctively wherever black men live together. They stand together and talk.

Bill's Song

Music came to Bill vicariously, free, and without a formal introduction. Every Saturday morning Ms. Eleanor in the apartment down the hall, opened her door and did her housecleaning to jazz music. Her loud music playing off her albums filled the entire building until she finished. The Band Shell in Colonial Park at 147th Street and Bradhurst sponsored big band concerts every summer. It was at the end of Bill's block, and the concerts were free. The Band Shell was Bill's first experience of being exposed to great musicians playing big band music, and it got his attention.

The Harlem riot in 1964 was a tragedy for some, but it was a jackpot for Bill because he got his first horn. Bill made a trade with a friend: a stolen watch, for a stolen horn, which came from a busted pawn shop window. Little did he know that the saxophone trade had no neck. Bill didn't care. He had a large piece of a horn, and he carried it around in a pillowcase.

Timing is everything.

The downtown move turned out to be a blessing in disguise. The Lower East Side was ripe with talented, serious musicians. He befriended Nelson Samiego, a magnificent sax player with enough self-confidence and bravado for several people. Through Nelson, Bill learned the value of self-disciplined, dedicated practice, and reading sheets. Nelson practiced all the time, like a man possessed.

In a neighboring housing project just steps away, in the Lillian Wald Houses, lived the jazz icon Jackie McClean and his son Rene. For the first time, Bill knew that it was possible for him to become a serious musician. An environment where being surrounded by talented men was, for Bill, likened to putting a dry sponge into a bucket of water. He was ready to expand his knowledge base and grow as a maturing young man. Bill could see the light at the end of the tunnel.

His new home on the Lower East Side and the village clubs were adjacent to each other and within walking distance. Fortunately for him, the village clubs were blasting with some of the best talent in the business. Giants like Kenny Durham, Booker Irving, Pharaoh Saunders, Archie Schepp, Wilbur Ware, Clifford Jordan, Bennie Maurpin, and Sun Ra were commonplace in the area. Now jazz had his attention, and he was more appreciative. Bill got rid of the pillowcase once Nelson introduced him to music stores. He saved his money weekly and completed his tenor saxophone with the purchase of a neck, mouthpiece, and an appropriate carrying case.

Finally a Horn of His Own

William Bill Saxton was finally on his way to becoming the somebody he envisioned: a jazz musician. But as his luck would have it, his Harlem teenage street activity from uptown caught up with him. His first and only conviction over a petty crime cost several years out his young life. Because his mother could not afford competent legal representation, her hard-to-come-by $300 bought her a warm body in a suit that barely showed up in court. Even though Bill was not dealing in drugs, didn't hurt anyone, had no prior record, and was a teen, he was convicted without a protest from his lawyer.

Again, fate had strange twist by dealing a positive hand in Bill's life. In Auburn State Penitentiary he met a serious jazz musician. The veteran inmate took the young, skinny teen under his wing. Bill now had a structured, uninterrupted time slot to learn skills and discipline; music was a perfect escape. He developed a love for practice and using time wisely. Separated from the outside world, the music of his friends Nelson and idols McClean, Rollins, Coltrane, and Shorter, remained constant in his head. Upon release, his vision for his future as a musician was grounded in cement.

The world had changed, as had Bill. Nothing was more dependable as his closely knit family. Because of his noticeably improved reading skills and his playing ability, his friendship with Nelson was enhanced, and they hit the village clubs. Nelson was a young, prodigious genius who was fearless to a fault. He was the perfect egotist that Bill needed to pump him up with super fuel, to try his fragile wings in the strong NYC jazz world of the 1960s and 70's.

Bill entered precisely where he needed to be in the world of jazz. Not only were the village clubs overflowing with creative giants, but he got the chance of a lifetime. Bill was able to get intense learning opportunities from two legendary icons of all times.

The first was in the late 1960s, with Clark Terry. With his own money, Clark created an opportunity for talented, inner-city youth to learn music and get skills needed to be good jazz musicians. Once Bill became a member, Bill's self-confidence as a professional musician began to gain momentum. With Clarks' strict direction, he improved in phrasing, articulating, and blending with sections of the band. Clarks' willingness to reach back to youth served as a template for Bill's generous, philosophical approach to helping the careers of young musicians.

Bill's second major career advancement was with Frank Foster and his big band. The mentorship bond between Frank and Bill grew very soon into a friendship. Frank's experience as a writer and arranger for over twenty years with Count Basie gave Bill personal experiences with the big band sound. Frank pushed Bill to trust his ability in improvisation by frequently featuring him as a lead saxophonist. Frank Foster opened a door to give Bill a chance to form a personal relationship with a much-needed, mature father figure and musical advisor.

Bill soon realized that most musicians had advanced training or had at least some college experience. He had a plan. The supervisor of his job, where he worked in a law office, had approached him about considering a law program seeking inner-city youth students. Bill mentioned his interest in attending a music school. His supervisor had a good friend, Guther Schuller, who happened to be the president of a music school. Bill was kissed by the gods again.

Guther Schuller was president of the New England Conservatory of Music in Boston. With their recommendation, Bill was granted a full scholarship to study music. Going off to college was terrifying. Bill solicited a friend from Harlem, Acey Sinclair, a trumpet player, to go along for support during registration. Both stayed in Boston and enrolled in the music program, and they received degrees from New England Conservatory.

However, Bill took a brief detour. In his senior year he auditioned for Mombo Santa Maria's band and was hired. He toured worldwide with the band, returned to Boston, and then finished his degree in music; he also earned a diploma in jazz studies, a new department. He and Sinclair Acey were among the original contributors to the virgin improvisational nature of the jazz program, initiated by Mr. Carl Atkins, Mr. George Russell, and Mr. Jackie Byard, who went on to establish the current New England Conservatory Jazz Program.

Bill's career path took him across the globe. His African travels alone included more than fifteen countries, where he had a chance to experience the cultural, tribal diversity across the vast continent. He was especially pleased to play at the North Sea Jazz Festival in Holland, in 1989. Anybody in the business who was highly recognized was there. It was his first time. After going to Sardinia, Italy, originally for a week but spending almost two months there, he realized that the growing trend of black jazz musicians moving to foreign countries for years at a time would not work for him; therefore, Germany, Spain, England, France, and other countries remained gigs instead of adventures. However, he never tired of Harlem.

The Capstone View

How I got to Bill's Place with Bill Saxton is as mysterious as trying to explain who he is now. The prism through which I see Bill's life is limited. I am biased and only perceive the man I met after all the hardcore work was hued out of the stone.

Those qualities that speak to what I know and see demonstrated daily appear across my stage with consistency and clarity. Bill is an unfinished mural on a wall in the schoolyard playground, full of young children yelling and screaming with joy and frustration. Bill is the tune that gets stuck in your head and drives you crazy until you either forget it or figure out its name. Since our lives have been intertwined for the last eleven years, I take ownership for a brief portion of the journey to our beloved Swing Street, and that is all. Life had pretty much softened him up for me, and at some point I planned to retire my hard hat and combat boots.

Harlem Hospital at 135th Street and Lenox Avenue,
where Bill was born

Bill's family home before the fire, 2534 Seventh
Avenue at 147th Street

Bill's family home before the fire, 2534 Seventh
Avenue at 147th Street

Bill's elementary school, PS 90

Band Shell, Robinson Park, West 148th Street and
Bradhurst Avenue, where Bill first heard live music

Band Shell, Jackie Robinson Park,
West 148th Street and Bradhurst Avenue where
Bill first heard live music

CHAPTER ELEVEN

Speaking Easy on Swing Street

Musicians who loved the uptown venues were forced to depend on and compete for gigs from an ever shrinking small pool of Harlem clubs. Eventually, all but a few of the old spots stayed open. Too few clubs were able to afford the escalating rents and quality musicians, and owners therefore began to hire young, inexperienced foreign musicians who worked for almost nothing, just to get a Harlem performance on their resumes. Low-balling by amateurs and the economic dilemma of club owners created a general lack of concern for high-quality music.

To keep their doors open, some owners began to hire inferior live talent, and some were reduced to hiring a DJ to spin records. The live jazz scene was beginning to dry up just as the neighborhoods began to improve. The more gentrified the neighborhood became, the more middle and upper class the residents became, and the higher the club leases became at renewal time. Unless one owned the property, one's business would at some point become too expensive to pass the costs on to the public and yield a profit.

In early 2001, the change in management at St. Nick's Pub proved to be the blessing in disguise. Although Bill had played the pub for ten years and established it as the best in jazz spot in Harlem, the break from the Saturday night ritual enabled him to renew his freedom by accepting gigs that required travel. However, we had begun to nurture our mutual dream to own a place, where we could create a unique performance environment. Locating a single space to satisfy our respective careers, was a monumental task.

What to Do?

The state of the economy during eight years of the Bush presidency was especially devastating for the arts communities. My natural instinct is to create from within, to go inside. Whatever is needed to fix the situation is there waiting to be discovered. Get your fingernails dirty and dig for the answer. Let's call it problem solving. Women are good at both ends: causing and curing problems. I was energized to find a cure. It was crucial to create an artistic endeavor that would satisfy the diverse artistic needs in the Harlem community. I did diligence to locate the perfect place for us.

Like a robot, I got up around 6:00 a.m. to start my real estate search. I was checking out the Internet and Craigslist for New York deals, as usual; it was my first stop of the day. My two-year search for the right Harlem property had become an early morning habit. I wanted location, location, location. Everything else was optional—after price, of course. The overpricing of property caused by gentrification was the force driving me. Bill and I needed the right place before the market soared out of reach.

As soon as the screen lit up, I saw a new listing. It read like an ad that I had placed. It spoke to the many particulars I was searching for, but most of all it had location. I responded by e-mail immediately; it didn't go through. Although it was early, I didn't care. I called and planned to leave a message. Surprisingly, the owner answered. After a brief talk, I knew that this was something that needed to be looked at right away. It seemed too good to be true, but I was willing to take a look anyway.

Getting Bill up at an early hour for any reason is a real challenge. He joined me, half-awake, for the site visit to 148 West 133rd Street, in the freezing cold at 7:00 a.m.

It's a Disaster

The place was everything I did not want. It could not have been worse. The building was too narrow, too dark, too cluttered, too old, and too neglected. The man had not bothered to clean the bathroom in years; the toilet was filled with rings of darkened, rancid stains in the once white enamel. Everything within sight was an ugly mess. A filthy awning was falling off the top of the entrance. The floors were grimy, but I could see an inch or two of decent hardwood peering around the square edge of the green metal file cabinet.

All it had was location.

Bill wanted to go home and go back to sleep. He left us and sat out front in his warm car. But for some reason, I wanted to pursue it. I ran from top to bottom several times and saw nothing encouraging, except a sturdy, watertight structure. The building seemed to be surviving in spite of its obvious neglect. It had an attitude, if that was possible. The obvious condition and price tag were equally repulsive, but there was something else that could not be logically explained, and it held my attention. Considering all of my property buying experiences, there was not one reason I could think of to consider taking it even as a free gift. In spite of everything, the building had a haunting feeling that spoke to me.

There was a familiar place in my memory's background of the St. Louis Thomas Street red brick row house. We had to pass through a narrow hallway and stairs to reach our upstairs flat. I knew I could have a relationship with the place and create whatever it was lacking. It felt comfortable. I had to ignore what I saw and went with my instinct. I took the leap, knowing the parachute would appear.

Bill trusted my ability to transform nothing into something and gave his guarded support. We made a preliminary offer on the spot. Bill was wide awake—money from his pocket is a sobering commodity for him. Newton made counteroffers, and Bill responded with more concessions. Eventually we locked in a good deal for the building that had nothing going for it with a very firm handshake.

Newton seemed more pleased to get rid of his tenant issues than he was with the less than perfect building. He had the big Kool-Aid smile of the salesman, who had just sold the deed to the Brooklyn Bridge. His sigh of relief was the obvious indication that we had our hands full. With a significant time delay, we eventually had a successful closing. It had been a rough trail to travel from the handshake on 133rd Street to the handing over of the deed in the attorney's West Side office.

Our work was cut out for us. Everything we suspected was wrong turned out to be worse. Every tenant in every apartment had a larger issue than we anticipated; the human drama they brought to our table was real and required constant attention. Our ownership of property had to include their conditions. It was a package deal.

The year 2005 began as a constant trail of setbacks and crisis. The boiler broke, the radiators leaked, toilets flooded, and the very large rats in the basement tried to take over the building. Amazingly, the only things that were not real problems were roaches and bedbugs; we had neither.

Having access to a private back yard in the heart of NYC, along with extra storage, was an attractive option for us. We were ready take control of our dreams. Bill would have his club for jazz music, and I would have space for book parties, poetry readings, and writing workshops. My dreams sounded good, but making

226

them happen was another story. The devil showed up in the detail to discourage our every move.

We knew that a giant transformation would have to take place for any real performance venue to materialize. What was a long, extremely narrow space that needed to accommodate many people supposed to look like? Most club prototypes in my mind were for larger and wider spaces. Our space was dismal. Bill's desire for the smallest baby grand piano was immediately out of the plan. My plan for a conference table was out.

At first there seemed to be no room for anything, but as small projects were done the space became more workable. Good vibes showed up.The wood floor was dirty but in reasonably good condition; it was solid and level, and it felt smooth under my heavy construction work boots. Natural light peeped in from each end of the oblong, awkward space. One large window in the front and one in the back gave equal sunlight to the abused but sturdy floor. The boards were holding on to warm and rustic brown hues of the honey maple, thin, flat slats that harmoniously laid one next to the other.

With an old broom with ill-shaped bristles (suffered from being used as a mop), a window support, and a door stop, I managed to shave away a layer or two of grit. The wood breathed; it had life left. The raw hard wood floor was the initial motivator. I approached it as a theater project: it was an empty stage in need of a set. I had to consider the bones of the foundation and the era of the construction. In 1910 the buildings of that time had parlors and sitting rooms. I decided to create a home setting for me and the unsettling spirits roaming around. I spent hours sitting, walking, measuring, and thinking on the old wood floors for several days. I had to be quiet to hear the footsteps. They were there. "Theda's Space," as I called it for a working title, would eventually end up as a warm and inviting space with a lovely parlor attitude. Based on faith, I had made the leap and knew I had to keep moving, making small steps, for the miracle to catch up. The unseen, rambling souls kept me company as I worked alone.

It was evident Bill's faith was thin. He needed to see a manifestation of something concrete he could feel good about in the midst of the ladders, paint cans, brushes, and tools. Although Bill never expressed his doubts, his apprehension was obvious. I had to always keep in mind that his creativity was wonderful, but it was for music and not the dirty work that accompanied interior design.

At times I was stuck, but I could not allow myself to be counted out. I had a crew of men to direct and work with daily. It was productive therapy. There was always something wrong on 133rd Street that needed my immediate, hands-on attention. I met the work crew at the building at 7:30 a.m. rain or shine for five months, shopped for materials and groceries with Bill at night, and slept when possible.

Bill helped when and where he could. He became an expert late-night shopper at Home Depot, and he kept the local street thugs and traffic away from our door. Bill's innate ability to handle himself with macho street savvy and "in your face" attitude was exactly what sustained us; we had a comfort zone with the regular boys hanging out on the block. Bill was in Harlem and at home. It gave safe passage for whoever entered the building.

Motion creates energy. When the large door was installed, it closed off the space and gave total privacy to our little space. Isolation was just what was needed. It was also dark. To create light, I covered the door in bright red and gold with splashes of black paint. Color combinations of reds and pink and purple and gold leaf on the wide moldings pumped life into the air. Piece by piece, wall by wall, the structure took on a life of its own and grew into the configuration we needed. Fixtures, took the persona of a period of long ago with mood lighting that reflected the feel of textured velvet. Shadows reflected off the beveled mirrors onto the adjacent walls of soft pink. In discrete corners, lingering cobwebs wavered under the breeze pushed against them by paint brushes spilling color across the masks of the past. Discarded pieces of bedposts, old shelves, and new Italian ceramic tiles came together in a small space, seemingly predisposed and determined to be the semblance of a fireplace in need of logs. Its mantel came to be the perfect nest to support the old dresser's mirror, left over in the basement.

Off of the kitchen floor, we nailed strong, precisely cut boards to hold the large flat plywood snugly to form the stage. Eventually, carpeting of rings of blue and gray would cover the last remains of kitchen, the heartbeat of the house.

Our shiny, black, new upright piano under bright lights made a statement of great expectations that was only upstaged by a comparable full set of drums. Once the stage was ready, Roy Haynes, the greatest living drummer, gave Bill a set of his signature drums, thereby christening the stage with full accreditation as a convener of jazz. Bill was elated to have the early support of Roy and the encouragement of Dr.

Billy Taylor in his pursuit to open a jazz venue of his own.

What's in a Name?

The name became a sticky point. What would we name it? Initially we wanted to include Harlem or Jazz or New York in the title. We were very strongly drawn to the Harlem Jazz Parlor at first. We looked at Theda and Bill's Place, but it felt too long. The lady gave up. Welcome to Bill's Place! (It's still Theda's Space.)

Theda and Bill Saxton

Life on Renewed Swing Street

During our first month on 133rd, a young man a few doors from us was killed by another young man across the street. They were neighbors, and their families had lived across the street from each other for many years. They were friends at some point. His death put an obvious strain on the street activity; the flow was stiff and guarded. Several months later, a young girl and another younger teenage boy were killed across the street from us, near the fire station. The two of them were close friends and were shot by someone they knew in the neighborhood after a brief argument. This time there was a different feel to the block. Faces showed less hostility and more sorrow.

The reality of losing two very young people familiar to everyone seemed to place a veil of sobriety to the loud music from windows of apartments and parked SUVs, the daylight craps games, and blunt smoking on the stoop. Almost instantly the block activity began to tone down, and self-corrective behavior became evident. "RIP" signs, pictures, and candles were on stoops on both sides of the street for months. It was like passing through a mausoleum of death, where the lives of murder victims were being held in high esteem along with teddy bears and flowers. Because of two different times and locations for the bodies, each side of the street alternated with display shrines of respect for their young, dead neighbors.

Based on my personal observations, the three youngsters who had been murdered spent a great deal of time standing around and leisurely hanging out on the stoop, talking, sitting, and looking up and down the street. It was as if they expected something new to happen on their block each day. I seldom saw them separately; they were tight. They were like faithful sentries watching at the walls of the castle. Although their demeanor was relaxed and comfortable, they always looking up and down the block. They seemed trapped in an out-of-date script in which their roles had been easily written out, without notification.

It was a hot summer that year. Buildings sat snugly side by side, preventing any air to breeze through. The tiny sidewalk space in front of the stoops and stairs was occupied by many very young teen mothers sitting or standing with their babies close by, while the baby carriages lined the sidewalk. All of the space was accounted for by the young block stakeholders; it was their turf.

The ladies on the stoops unbraided and braided hair constantly. Often the inexpensive hair bought at the

Korean beauty supply store on the Avenue would get find its way into a small pile and blow around in air funnels up and down the street. Sometimes the wads of hair would become airborne and land in my flower boxes or up on the next corner, near the juice bar. But the bottom line was that the neatly, intricately designed curves and angles of braids made the head of the wearer look like a Nubian goddess for a few weeks. No one cared where the synthetic hairballs went. The 133rd Street people lived on their block, and the sidewalks served the deck to the patio of their urban front yards. Death was just another part of their living while waiting and watching for something to happen, hoping for something good to appear.

The RIP memorials framed the action of the days that followed until hot sun and a heavy rain reduced the shrine to a trash pile collected by the building super and discarded in the trash can. The ink of pictures adorning the RIP banner streaked tears of black down the limp paper falling from the side of the wall that served as the designated location of the expressions of sorrow. The NYC sanitation garbage trucks squashed the small shrines and pressed them in tight for the long ride to the landfills at some desolate location, along with the other litter and black plastic garbage bags from Swing Street.

235

Mourning time was over, and gentrification was alive, well, and moving in fast on a block still grappling with the unhappy ghosts of black residents from almost a century past. Black residents of Swing Street, old and new, were forced to accept their neighborhoods and to unconditionally absorb the activities of white people with money. During the last century, their block was invaded in the name of Prohibition and now they were being replaced by gentrification. The rhetorical question for the current generation of Swing Street black stakeholders should be, "What about us?"

God places you where you are supposed to be; just shut up, roll up your sleeves, and do his work.

I decided to offer a little beauty to my small area next door. I planted flower boxes of bright red geraniums along our fence bordering the sidewalk, and I placed pots of petunias in the yard near the entrance. I was a part of the block, too, and would contribute my lifestyle along with theirs and make the setting reflect our range of lifestyles. When I came out to water or pick off dead buds, the glances and smiles of the stoop crew became more frequent, and by the end of summer we were speaking.

Six days a week throughout the hot summer, I worked to clean up behind the excavation crew, who had removed the old refrigerators, tires, furniture, and car parts to fill the dumpster out front. Daily I faced twenty years of garbage left from the carnage of a slum landlord, but change was in the air. I would plant my own beautiful rose garden there. Getting the ground leveled off and cleaned up would take another full week of sifting out the broken glass and syringes and crack vials. By fall, it was ready for a few potted plants near the door, which could finally remain open. It became the perfect, quiet retreat from the countless other tasks required to whip a hundred-year-old building into shape. The place started to come together inside and out.

Inside, shades of red, gold, and lavender dominated the color palette and wonderfully served the framed artwork hanging from the vibrant walls. Faces and lyrics of musicians floated in and out and about on the breeze of the ceiling fan, revealing smiles, fleeting eyes, and music. There was always a sense of music scanning the fabulous, too-narrow, too-long space with jazz bravado. Music spilled out at every turn in the midst of days and years gone by, not forgotten. It felt like home.

Like magic the atmosphere of the 1920s and 1930s showed up, ready to be seen and heard. Everything fell into place like a staged set in one of my Lincoln

U stage crafter classes under Dr. T. D. Pawley. The project turned out to be exactly what was desired. We were fulfilled with pride and satisfaction to see the physical manifestation of our dream.

Payday

Bill received the early support of many friends who were famous jazz greats. The late John Hicks, my homeboy, was the first person to play our pretty, new, shiny black piano. He said it had a full and good sound; Bill was pleased. Hicks and Andy McCloud came immediately to see and play in the club before it opened. They were excited for Bill and for the possibilities it would offer to jazz musicians.

We opened December 2, 2005, at the beginning of the Christmas holiday season and a harsh winter. It was the wrong time to open a new business. In our eagerness to get started, we acted prematurely. It was devastating. Our timing was off, but Bill's stubborn determination was undaunted. Our first staff members, Tracey and Monika Webb, were the trailblazers along with our friend, the house manager, Sinclair Acey. Sinclair's presence gave us two crucial ingredients. Not only was he a wonderful trumpet player, Acey had a trained musician's ear for professional artistic feedback and a no-nonsense attitude for the overall demeanor of the club. By the second year Rachelle Reyes, became our hostess, and created the warm, professional atmosphere that made every night a class act. Kenny "Spider" Webb, the golden voice of WBLS for many years, graced our small stage and gave more polish to our show.

In the first couple of years, oftentimes the quality of the music was higher than the number of people in the audience, but every performance was worthy of a standing ovation for our primarily white patrons. The initial scarcity of the numbers did not affect the integrity of the musicians' attitude toward their craft. Audiences were impressed with the quality of the performances and the warmth of the environment. The numbers increased.

However, numbers are meaningless if the count is the focus. Our immediate Harlem neighbors remained observers. Neither our open invitations nor our street outreach block parties could get them to cross our doorstep. They extended polite conversation but made no attempt to socially associate with us. Bill's Place may as well had been labeled off limits for them as they watched our clientele increase and listened to the jazz flood the narrow sidewalks.

White Women Back in the House, Again!

Ironically, it was white women, and a few white men, who consistently showed up since the beginning to support and enjoy the music. As if a playback, the racial and gender composition of our speakeasy audience was identical to a Harlem nightlife scene from the segregation days of the 1920s or 1930s. Some sets were exclusively white, except for the black men in the band; the house was mostly white. Between sets, socializing, drinking, and smoking in the garden was for the most part jazz-loving white customers.

In the first couple of years, it bothered me tremendously; my racial pride suffered then and now. We went to hell and back to have a place that was a comfort zone for everyone. I became diligent in calling, mailing, and networking my black contacts and networks. With no or limited response from local and regional black customers, I stopped direct appeals.

I have to believe that black people love jazz. It is the way it presented that makes the difference uptown. Listening to jazz, socializing, and buying drinks at a bar has historically been the preferred Harlem social culture. Old bars of the past, like the Baby

Grand and Smalls, had huge bars, and jazz music, and large black crowds packed the place primarily to drink. Their customers bought drinks at the same place they socialized.

Our speakeasy setting is different, and the cultural and racial divide attached to Swing Street is unfortunately as valid now as it was in 1923. Consequently, I am no longer annoyed with black male jazz musicians who are with white women. Oftentimes, I am the only black woman present.

The historical documentation, of the social interracial relationship between the availability of white women, with black male jazz musicians and celebrities is very much unchanged in seventy-five years. I will not begin to touch upon the denial of the "light to white" color preference of women by older and younger black accomplished men, because that would take forever and a day of open combat.

I'm still hopeful for my gentrified block. Maybe one day they'll accept the invitation to leave their stoop for just an evening, to venture across our nearby doorway, to enjoy their own live black music where it flourished during the Jazz Era. Little do they know that it is their unique flavors and style that keeps our Harlem treasure culturally real as Swing Street.

The separation of the unspoken class distinctions still appear to be at work. Maybe my young stoop neighbors will bless me with their presence and come inside for once, to the book signing, and autograph my copy. It's been eight years trying to make a connection.

CHAPTER TWELVE

Our Angel, Charlie

Charlie Phillips, one of Bill's close friends and a neighbor, taped an envelope to the door one morning, with a simple notation written in perfect calligraphy: "This should interest you." Enclosed were pages from the *New York Press*, November 16-22, 2005. The front-page headline read, "The Rise and Fall of Swing Street: How Prohibition helped Harlem get Jazzed," by David Freeland. The entire article was about our block on West 133rd Street, between Lenox and Seventh Avenues.

Our new property acquisition was featured explicitly. The small building, at 148 West 133rd Street, was given historical perspective. We were shocked at the revelation. Charlie was singularly responsible for us knowing our historic connection with the past and the engine that fueled my research to write this book.

Fate was in my visual design. It was fortuitous that all creative energy forces led back to the appropriate 1920s era in my Harlem décor and attitude. It was a supernatural relationship for me from the very beginning. The ease in which all the pieces pulled together and created a harmonious setting was always like predesigned patterns. It was meant to come back to life. That was the "something" I was drawn to the first day. It was very powerful and kept my attention. The renovations were like a step back into a classic Vanderzee Harlem parlor photograph. How perfectly logical, but who knew? Do spirits give voice to others across time?

The late Charlie Phillips was an intellectual mentor who deftly used humor to connect social issues with minimal intrusion. Charlie Phillips was an information junkie. He went back to college and got his bachelor's degree when he was past seventy-five. He knew something of value about almost anything one wanted to know, and he could answer in a succinct one liner. His wit was always poignant. Charlie's glib, tongue-in-cheek communication style always kept one on guard for the punch line.

It took a while for either of us to bother to read the three-page article, but after we did, our interests as owners of Bill's Place moved up to a higher level of cultural consciousness and community responsibility to Harlem. Charlie put us on Swing Street.

Bill's Place was no longer about being a part of the wave of the new gentrification to own real estate; we were grounded in American history, which eventually affected life on our Harlem block.

In 2004, for no logical reason, I was strangely attracted to the building at 148 West 133rd Street. Now that this small research project put the trail of women in my mind, I am clear about my place in the process. I believe a spirit or a ghost spoke to me; once Charlie Phillips pulled our coat to the real deal surrounding Bill's Place, it made sense. Charlie connected the dots. The ghosts needed a host agent to complete the cycle.

All life begins with inhaled air (birth), and it stops with exhaled air (death). Your spirit's soul or life is breaths of air living in structures called bodies. Your last breath goes into the universe and lives there, to be used over and over again. Air is where the spirit moves about to continue working at whatever it does. I showed up, and so did the roaming, unsettled spirits. The rest is history. Tillie's ghost invaded my roots to reconnect an unfinished historical era, and to rejuvenate the speakeasy and place live jazz at its core. But its past owner, Ms. Moore, had an unhappy energy that held me hostage. She was unknown to me.

Ms. Monette Moore had been cheated from her rightful place in jazz history as a major player in the stardom of Billie Holiday. Her name never shows up as the essential link between Billie and fame. My angel Charlie probably knew I would dig her out of the rubble and polish up her image for all to see, with appreciation and compassion for her life's destiny in the jazz world.

According to several Harlem historical documents and resources, Ms. Monette Moore was a very popular singer and performer. In 1933 she billed to appear at the Harlem Opera House along with the widely acclaimed actor Charles Muse. Monette was very popular with white and black audiences, and she was known to have an excellent voice and radiant personality. Local papers frequently had pictures of her on stage. She was a dark brown-skinned woman with average features and with a body build reminiscent of the famous Mamie Smith. It is rumored that a Hollywood star, Clifton Webb, and a local gangster financed her to take over and open a spot at 148 West 133rd Street. She reopened Tillie's Fripp and Conan's former place, and she named the tiny speakeasy Monette's Supper Club.

Late one evening in 1933, her club was bustling with activity, and Monette was busy socializing and hosting her adoring guests. She was especially anxious to shower attention on many important white men from the music industry who were invited by her to observe her showcase performance. In order to give her important guests personal attention, she invited a young, unknown local teenage girl who was always up and down the street canvassing the clubs looking for a gig, to fill in for her with the band as an opening act.

John Hammond, the well-connected white promoter, was seated in the audience. He was impressed with the stand-in teenager's voice and appearance. Although Hammond had come in to hear Monette, his interest in Monet immediately paled, and he actively sought the attention of his new discovery. The unknown teen girl turned out to be Billie Holiday. He instantly became her agent and booked her gigs, and in two years secured Billie a recording contract. Destiny took over for both women.

Unfortunately, Hammond's interest in Monette never peaked. He was grateful to Ms. Moore for her having Billie there at the same time he happened to have been in her club, but he had found the singer he wanted to back. Monette was devastated and was helpless to compete with the younger, beautiful, light-skinned talent with the unusual voice.

Three weeks later, Monette Moore closed with a broken spirit. She thought she was doing no one a favor, and it turned out to be her professional suicide in Harlem. Not only did she miss an opportunity for herself, but she was also given no credit for providing the opportunity for Billie to be heard and discovered by John Hammond. She was the sacrifice in 1933.

Ms. Moore's spirit needed my voice for her resolution and praise. Thank you, Ms. Monette Moore, for giving a desperate young girl a chance to sing at the right place and at the right time.

Timing is everything.

Aging has taught me how little I know about the mysteries of life. There are forces that place you where you are at a given time, for seemingly unexplainable reasons. But sometimes we need to be still, get quiet, listen, and then take the leap of faith, knowing there will be a safe landing. How else would I have known to decorate in detail, as if directed by a 1920s interior designer of a movie set for Fats Waller or Mamie Smith? I was spirit led from the morning

I first walked in until I hung the last lace curtain before we opened.

Spirits had been stuck in limbo almost seventy-five years, waiting for me to show up and complete their story. On Saturday, October 6, 2012, we invited the family and friends of Charlie's over to Bill's Place for a dedication celebration. Bill and I set aside a space called "Charlie's Jazz Corner" and placed his picture and plaque in his honor on the wall, adjacent to a picture of Louis Armstrong. Charlie's spirit is now a part of Swing Street in Bill's Place. By way of his insistence to have the truth known to us, he is now involved in ways only known to him years ago. The spirit of Charlie has been swept across the floor boards and has landed on the walls to perch, in the catbird seat, to keep an eye on us and create peace for the ghosts lulling around the parlor from time to time. I'm sure that the ghosts of Tillie and Billie and Monette will find Charlie a strange piece of work to visit with, now that he has the only official status and in-house residency in Bill's Place.

Charlie enabled us to appropriately refer to our site as
Bill's Place, Harlem's authentic Speak Easy,
148 west 133rd street, Village of Harlem.
On this day, October 6th 2012, we dedicate this space as

Charlie's Jazz Corner

with love
Bill and Theda Saxton

Charlie Phillips

CHAPTER THIRTEEN

Bill and Bebop Are At Home in Harlem

Bill is a serious and consistent musician who received total respect and output from his young band because he gave 100 percent each time he put his horn in his mouth. His determination to play the music as it deserved to be played, no matter what, endeared him to his meager, initial audiences. Bill's Harlem Jazz Band played world-class music for each and every show. The club never closed because of poor attendance or bad weather. The band got better, and so did the reputation of Bill's Place. The best advertising, by word of mouth, was how Bill's Place became sustainable. Pianist, Theo Hill, drummer Jason Brown and Dave Gibson and bass player, Zaid Shukri and Dave Jackson were the pioneer musicians who set the elevated bar with Bill that is a quality standard.

Enthusiastic jazz fans told others about the music and the rare mystique of the homey feeling and 1920s Harlem motif. Phone calls began to trickle in from tourists and foreigners surfing the Internet for an exciting night out listening to jazz in Harlem. The unique, personalized, intimate traits of Bill's Place, coupled with dependable world-class jazz led by Bill, was the selling point. The music brought them in, and the ambiance embraced them. Its reputation received a coveted 5 star rating from YELP before long.

Too many times, it is forgotten that this wonderful music is made by each musician's contribution. Bill's Place is an advocate of free expression of those who make the music. I was curious to hear from some of those who are directly responsible as contributors to the current success of Bill's Place. We are only as good as the quality of the music that is played at the next show.

Here are some personal comments made by a few musicians.

Bobby Watson

Bill brings a deep love and respect for the community. Being born and raised in Harlem, his sense of history is unparalleled. He is sincere. He is a world-class musician and recording artist who brings a deep understanding and simpatico to the club. This is truly unique.

I believe that clubs like Bill's Place, where the artist has control of the venue and program, is the way of the future. I am also sure that others will try to franchise the idea to take advantage of the resurgence of the Harlem community. But I would hope that black entrepreneurs will see the historic as well as the financial value of owning a jazz club.

Dave Jackson

I see the future of Harlem jazz clubs surviving on the dollars of people who live outside of the Harlem community. The young people particularly are less likely to attend venues. A large segment of the pop culture is so removed from the fundamentals of music such as melody, rhythm, harmony, and composition that jazz is not appreciated.

They have grown up in a period of mediocrity—that is, sampling real music and gradual replacement of musicians with computerized sounds. The foundation of blues and gospel, which were imminent spiritual forces of jazz origins and traditions, are relatively absent in current musical styles.

Dave F. Gibson

Bill Saxton brings to the Harlem jazz community artistry, honesty, dedication, humility, and excellence. Mr. Saxton believed that the only way to play music he has written and use the musicians he wants is to open his own jazz club. I remember when Bill was working at St. Nick's Pub every Friday night for ten years, to a guaranteed packed house.

From time to time, Bill has had other musicians play in place of him and use their own musicians for the band. We jumped at the idea. We know that it is a good idea for a musician to own the club. It is not about the money; we just want to preserve the music that deserves to be back on commercial radio.

I hope Bill's Place remains a source of jazz in the Harlem community, because it is where you can come and hear great music at a reasonable price, and not be forced out at the end of the set or made to pay an additional cover charge.

T. K. Blue

Serious jazz in Harlem is in serious trouble.

Unless we find a way to have more venues and make them more affordable and accessible to the local community, we remain in trouble. There is currently a problem to get more African Americans, especially the young people, to come out and support jazz venues in Harlem. It's truly a current paradox because historically, jazz had a huge following in Harlem from "back in the day" of Minton's, Smalls Paradise, Monroe's Uptown House, Lucky Roberts (St. Nick's Pub), Lenox Lounge, and many more.

Musicians need to find a way to make jazz music more appealing to the younger generation without compromising their integrity. In addition, we need to find ways to keep this indigenous art form in the community that nurtured its development and innovations.

Dion Parsons

Bill Saxton was born in Harlem, was raised in Harlem, and developed his musicianship with Harlem's best musicians in the world. He represents Harlem in everything he does. As the owner of Bill's Place, he has established himself as the cornerstone for the jazz community. He has presented his club in the tradition of the speakeasies that once flourished in New York City. His idea of having the audience right there with the band creates an atmosphere that is very intimate and real. One can reach out and touch the audience; this promotes an exciting time for everyone.

Bill has also made it a point of nurturing up-and-coming musicians that need to learn from a master musician. His approach to music is direct and different from what one would find in any jazz ensemble class at any university. Bill Saxton is a true testament of jazz in Harlem.

Marco Digennaro

The first time I came to Bill's Place, I was really scared to play with musicians on such a high level. It was my first time to play in New York. He did not know me and called for an F blues, which immediately put me at ease. I feel comfortable in Bill's Place. Bill brings his love and skills to his music.

I was raised in Italy, a country with a jazz-less culture. Having the possibility to make music with people like Bill, who comes out of the inner part of jazz music history, is like a dream. I am learning to respect the Harlem culture and my own unique, melodic Italian background. I have this to bring to jazz music.

Bill is a generous man for doing what he does at Bill's Place. He pays out of his pocket, because he knows that money is not the main issue—it's the music. Every musician receives respect no matter the skill level, as long as he shows respect for the music, and of course Bill. He allows everyone to bring something to the table.

I am very appreciative to be in Harlem, the place where it all happened for this music. This is where I dedicate myself as a musician. The walls of Bill's Place absorbed the vibes then, and now they give them back.

Patience Higgins

To the community, for a musician to be the owner of his own club means we see a person who has not only earned the respect of his peers as a quintessential musician, but who has achieved the dream of most: to own one's own club. It's an accomplishment admired by all.

Hearing instruments acoustically for musicians and audiences is the main difference that one experiences in Bill's Place. The ability to personally interact with people is very rewarding for both musician and audience.

CHAPTER FOURTEEN

God Bless the Child ... as told by Bill Saxton

When I was almost three years old, I remember trying to look out the window of our living room. It was a wide window with a deep stone ledge that always felt cool to my hands on hot days. The window was a popular place; everybody kept pulling the curtains aside while looking and sometimes shouting out. I was held in my mother's lap or by Marie's hand, but today no one was around, and I decided to see the outside on my own.

As I crawled up, I could see the sky. Then as I got out to the end of the ledge, I could see top floor windows of 2533, the building across the street. And then I realized I was out there alone and didn't know how to get back. Miraculously, my godfather, Jim, grabbed me by the legs and probably saved my life. Needless to say I got a good spanking; now this is called child abuse, but it cured me of wanting to climb onto the windowsill. I didn't do that again, but my desire to see and do life on my own terms has not changed.

I've been a fully grown man for many years now, but I keep crawling, stepping, running, and climbing onto unknown places. Seeking the unfamiliar and testing myself seems to go hand in hand with this wonderful music; it's always a new adventure. I have lived it to the best of my ability, and I'm still learning, still practicing. To do the music, to do jazz, is my life. Now the world stage kicks my ass.

Luck is the corner where preparation and opportunity meet, and you must know to capture it and use the moment. I have been blessed to have had many of these opportunities along the way. I am standing on the shoulders of many great musicians. So many have given to me the proper preparation to move forward and grow in the music.

Please join me in my pictorial journey as I pay homage to the music and those who have given to me the best hands-on training any musician can ever hope to have. I have selected these particular memorable events to give you an understanding of my professional growth in becoming the musician and businessman I am today.

Jazz icons and legends Clark Terry and Frank Foster bestowed upon me the privilege of their consistent presence over the majority of my professional life. Combined, their gift to the music is not possible to record or quantify in historical importance.

Letter written to Bill, May 20, 2011

Dear Bill,

We first met when Bill was about 19 or 20 at the Jazz Club La Boheme located at Broadway at 66th St. in NYC. I was rehearsing a 10-piece band for an engagement there, and needed a tenor saxophonist. Bill was there and sat in, but couldn't play or read well. Desperate to fill the chair, I hired him despite his obvious limitations.

Bill had attended some workshops at Jazz Interactions, an organization founded by trumpeter, Joe Newman. I'm sure this experience helped in Bill's development as a musician. I was an instructor there, but I didn't teach Bill.

While later attending the New England Conservatory of Music, Bill applied for and got a grant to study privately with me at my home in South Ozone Park (Queens) N.Y. because, he says, after hearing me play he became a disciple of mine. Whenever Bill came back to town, he worked with me in whatever band I had at the time ... I always had a band of some type ... 10 pcs, 12 pcs, 18 pcs, 23 pcs. Cecilia managed me and my bands' and made us all one big family. Respective degrees of raw talent notwithstanding.

Bill and Danny Mixon were seemingly more needy than the rest, musically and family-wise, and were with me as often as they could be. I began to refer to them both as my sons and still do. They call me "Pop."

When I had my stroke in 2001 and realized that I'd probably never play my tenor sax again, I told Bill I would leave it to him in my will. After 9 years, to help me with my expenses, Bill just bought the horn from me.

At times, as Bill's playing progresses, he often sounded a lot like me, but then he began developing his own style. That's the way of the world … the youngsters grow up and grow out. I couldn't be more proud of his accomplishments, music-wise and business-wise.

Carry on, son.

Frank Foster

On July 26, 2011, the legendary jazz giant Dr. Frank Benjamin Foster III went down swinging. At his funeral at the Oak Grove Methodist Church in Chesapeake, Virginia, on stage just behind the brier, I stood alone and represented the members of his beloved Loud Minority Band, and played a piece of Frank's original music solo. "Simone" was so powerfully melodic that it seemed to fill every square inch of the gothic hall. As it ended, his daughter, Andrea, whom I have known all of her life, sprung to her feet with arms raised in praise of her father's work, and she hugged me. The raw honesty of the moment humbled me. Pops's music lived.

Jazz goes on. The music is so rich and deep that it continues no matter how great the loss. I have found that when the music world seems to dim, there is always another source to brighten the scene in a different way. Recently the jazz community has been blessed to have a permanent document and historically significant account of a life in the jazz world for over fifty years, written by one of the most prolific musicians of all times. *Clark,* the autobiography of Mr. Clark Terry, represents the ultimate contribution to the world of valuable books. It gives a full picture of a man overcoming difficulties that were inevitable in the life of a devoted jazz musician in an entertainment industry designed with an uneven playing field for African Americans. I was proud to be remembered by Clark, where he recalled his years spent educating the Harlem tough guys, as he called us. Reading the pages pulled me back in time to with him and situations as if it were yesterday. On pg. 193 he explains his task with us,

> I taught them how to read music and all about phrasing. How to solo and how long to solo. The particulars of music theory. Notations, quotations, chords and progressions. They learned to play a big band book, and looked over their arrangements. Encouraged them just like I'd done with Q [Quincy Jones].

We got so much from him, and it's good to know that it wasn't a one-way street and that Clark got some pleasure from us. "It was one of the best feelings in the world to see the joy on their faces. They had a lot of potential and made a lot of progress." He further iterates his feelings about the group of young Harlem musicians he sponsored with his own money and other professional resources. "Watching the young cats in that Harlem youth band grow into their own careers made me feel proud. They were like family to me. "I had to make sure I did my part to continue perpetuating jazz". Further on the same page, he blew my mind: "Bill Saxton became a regular in my Big Bad Band, as well as a successful independent musician and the owner of his own club in Harlem" (p. 194).

What an honor. Having Clark Terry to acknowledge me as having an important place in his life, and as being a successful musician, serves as my professional report card. From the beginning, he encouraged me to live my dream in Harlem with the opening of a jazz venue. Bill's Pace perpetuates the lives of all of us in the profession. He and Frank Foster provided me with the role models I needed as a young musician trying to find a voice in the world of jazz. Equally as important is the fact that I was able to have a jazz venue of my very own during their lifetimes. Bill's Place speaks for a whole generation of cats who pioneered and laid the groundwork for live jazz, and didn't have blessings fall right to have a business themselves. Frank and Clark were a part of my life, and they have a direct link to the spot, but Hawkins, Parker, Coltrane, and all the ghosts of past giants kept me on my feet and kept my spirits up during the lowest moments over the past years.

It has not been an easy road to consistently maintain an honest art form so that the Harlem fingerprint I leave on this music venue is deserving of those who make the music authentic and relevant for the future of jazz in the African American culture and the world. I was born two blocks from here. It's taken over sixty-seven years to get from there to here on Swing Street with my Harlem Bebop Band. But I'm here.

End of Set

Bill's Encore

At this time I'd like to introduce the stars who have been showing up with me over the past forty years at one gig or another. Every time I put my horn in my mouth to blow a note, I pull from my time spent with them and their music. It is their presence that shows up and fills the empty spaces between these sacred walls of old plaster and cement here in Harlem, setting fire to the scene. When they show up, I can almost fly. Some nights the spirit gets so strong in the place that it's like church. It's electric.

The cats fill up the place and give me what I need to say, in the special way I'm always searching to express the next idea that eats away at my insides. I play a small part in a long, solid chain of giant golden links. Here they are.

Bill Saxton and Sonny Stitt

Max Roach and Bill Saxton

Barry Harris, Willie Williams, Clark Terry,
Carrie Smith, and Bill Saxton

Sonny Rollins and Bill Saxton

Bill Saxton, Jackie McClean, and Gary Bartz

Pharaoh Saunders and Bill Saxton

Lionel Hampton and Bill Saxton

Bill Saxton and Illinois Jacquet

Tito Puente and Bill Saxton

Bill Saxton and Oscar Peterson

Joe Williams and Bill Saxton

Dr. Frank Foster

The Last Call

It's Time to Tally Up and Get on Our Way

Jazz has continued to be woven into the Harlem infrastructure of Swing Street, from the old muddy cotton fields and dilapidated juke joints to the polished ballroom floors. It survives. Most of all, first and foremost, Bill's Place has become home for exemplary jazz to happen in its purest form: improvisation. Bill Saxton has carried the building blocks of commitment on his back each Friday for eight years to maintain a standard of excellence for himself, his audience, and most of all for the future of black America's music.

The people who come through the red door are fans for life. They come back and bring friends and family. They know they have finally heard jazz in Harlem, the way they thought it ought to be played. They've had the "music in your face" relationship with the musician. It's always different and grows as it goes along.

I wonder if those busy ladies out in Ohio over 135 years ago would have done what they did to get Prohibition passed if they had known the staggering consequences. Thanks to them, Harlem got speakeasies on Swing Street, and all the drama and jazz that went with the era. Now it's up to gentrification to put its spin on the village and see what it will bring. Who's protecting Harlem's valuable history from the embracing arms of gentrification? The answer to that is another adventure for the next ghosts to conjure.

Rachelle, it's time for you to say what you always say so nicely,

"Good night, and thanks for coming to Bill's Place."

Resources

Badger, Reid. *A Life in Ragtime*. New York: Oxford University Press, 1995.

Burns, Ken, and Jeffrey C. Ward. *Jazz History of America's Music*. New York: Random House, 2000.

Bynum, Lee. "Harlem's Continuing Gentrification and Intraracial Relations." Published as part of a USA Rise Up Magazine's National Collegiate Dialogue Series on Race Relations.Columbia Teachers College NY, Academia, 2013.

Clark, Terry. *The Autobiography of Clark Terry with Gwen Terry*.Berkeley:University of California Press, 2011.

Clarke, Donald. *Billie Holiday, Wishing on the Moon*. Cambridge: DeCapo Press, 2002.

Colin, Paul. *Josephine Baker and La Revue Negre*. New York: Harry N. Abrams, Inc., 1998.

Dale, Rodney. *The World of Jazz*. USA: Elsevier-Dutton, 1980.

De Veaux, Lexis. *Don't Explain*. New York: Writers and Readers Publishing, Inc., 1988.

Dougherty, David. "Columbia U.: Race, Class and the Gentrification of Harlem." Taken from typed transcript of news carried on broadcast, The Real News Network, July 24, 2011.

Frost, William J., Donna L. Robert, Howard C. Kee, and Carter Lindberg. *Christianity: A Social and Cultural History*. 2nd ed. New Jersey: Prentice Hall, 1988.

Gill, Jonathan. *Harlem*. New York: Grove Press, 2011.

Goldstein, Rhoda L., ed. *Black Life and Culture in the United States*. New York: Thomas Y. Crowell Company, 1971.

Hirschfeld, Al. *Hirschfeld's Harlem*. New York: Glenn Young Books, 2004.

Huggins, Irvin Nathan. *Harlem Renaissance*. New York: Oxford University Press, 1971.

Ianni, Francis A. J. *Black Mafia: Ethnic Succession in Organized Crime*. New York: Simon and Schuster, Inc., 1974.

Leman, Nicholes. *The Promised Land*. New York: Random House, 1992.

Lewis, David Levering. *When Harlem Was in Vogue*. *New York:* Oxford University Press, 1979.

Okrent, Daniel. *Last Call: The Rise and Fall of Prohibition*. New York: Simon and Schuster, 2010.

O'Meally, Robert. *Lady Day*. New York: Arcade Publishing, 1991.

Schoener, Allon, ed. *Harlem on My Mind*. New York: Random House, 1968.

Terborg-Penn, Rosalyn. *African American Women in the Struggle for the Vote, 1850-1920*. Bloomington: Indiana University Press, 1998.

Weatherford, Carole Boston. *Becoming Billie Holiday*. Honesdale, PA: Wordsong, 2008.

CPSIA information can be obtained
at www.ICGtesting.com
Printed in the USA
FFHW021026141118
49395060-53720FF